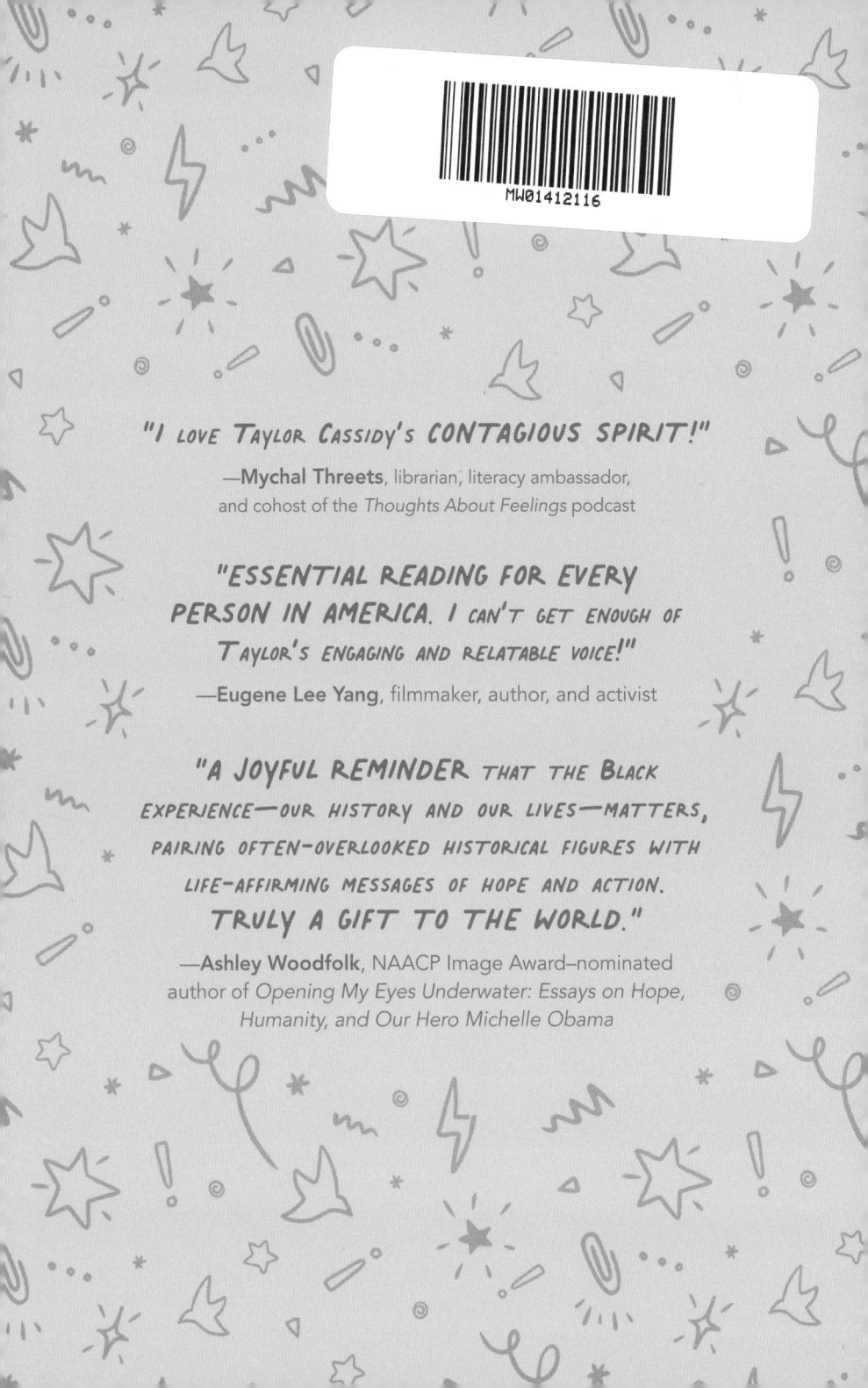

"I LOVE TAYLOR CASSIDY'S CONTAGIOUS SPIRIT!"

—**Mychal Threets**, librarian, literacy ambassador, and cohost of the *Thoughts About Feelings* podcast

"ESSENTIAL READING FOR EVERY PERSON IN AMERICA. I CAN'T GET ENOUGH OF TAYLOR'S ENGAGING AND RELATABLE VOICE!"

—**Eugene Lee Yang**, filmmaker, author, and activist

"A JOYFUL REMINDER THAT THE BLACK EXPERIENCE—OUR HISTORY AND OUR LIVES—MATTERS, PAIRING OFTEN-OVERLOOKED HISTORICAL FIGURES WITH LIFE-AFFIRMING MESSAGES OF HOPE AND ACTION. TRULY A GIFT TO THE WORLD."

—**Ashley Woodfolk**, NAACP Image Award–nominated author of *Opening My Eyes Underwater: Essays on Hope, Humanity, and Our Hero Michelle Obama*

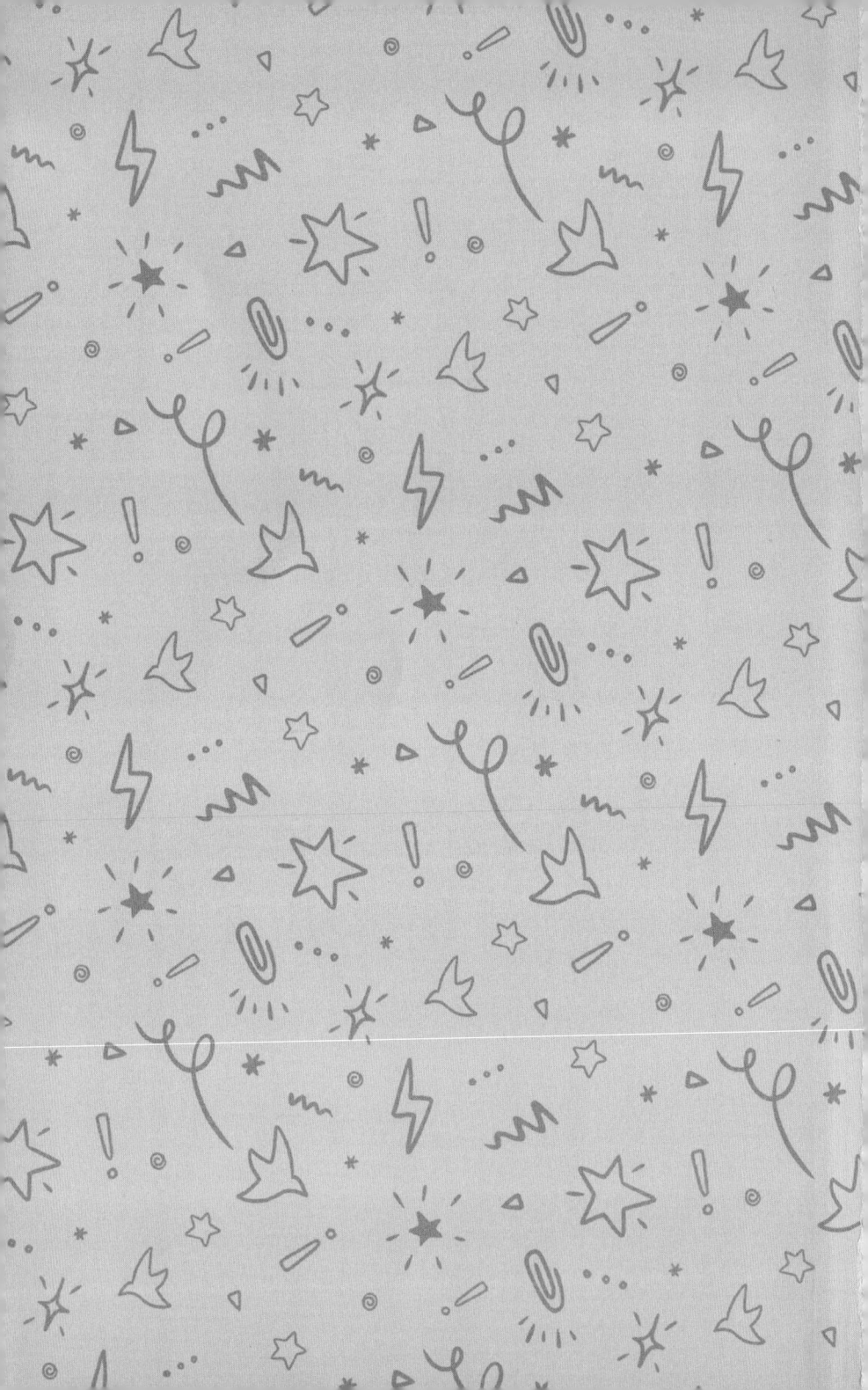

BLACK HISTORY IS YOUR HISTORY

TAYLOR CASSIDY

BLACK HISTORY IS YOUR HISTORY

ILLUSTRATED BY ADRIANA BELLET

atheneum

NEW YORK   AMSTERDAM / ANTWERP   LONDON
TORONTO   SYDNEY / MELBOURNE   NEW DELHI

atheneum

An imprint of Simon & Schuster Children's Publishing Division
1230 Avenue of the Americas, New York, New York 10020
For more than 100 years, Simon & Schuster has championed authors and the stories they create. By respecting the copyright of an author's intellectual property, you enable Simon & Schuster and the author to continue publishing exceptional books for years to come. We thank you for supporting the author's copyright by purchasing an authorized edition of this book.

No amount of this book may be reproduced or stored in any format, nor may it be uploaded to any website, database, language-learning model, or other repository, retrieval, or artificial intelligence system without express permission. All rights reserved. Inquiries may be directed to Simon & Schuster, 1230 Avenue of the Americas, New York, NY 10020 or permissions@simonandschuster.com.

This work is in part a memoir. It reflects the author's present recollections of her experiences over a period of years.

Text © 2025 by Taylor Cassidy
Jacket and interior illustration © 2025 by Adriana Bellet
Jacket design by Rebecca Syracuse
Interior illustration by LysenkoAlexander/iStock (paper memo); ainsel/iStock (scroll banner); lineartestpilot/iStock (pocket watch); Polina Tomtosova/iStock (sparks and threaded needle); Anatolii Kovalov/iStock (penciled arrows and lines); Anastasiia Hevko/iStock (scribbles and penciled circles and lines)
All rights reserved, including the right of reproduction in whole or in part in any form.
Atheneum logo is a trademark of Simon & Schuster, LLC.
For information about special discounts for bulk purchases, please contact Simon & Schuster Special Sales at 1-866-506-1949 or business@simonandschuster.com.
Simon & Schuster strongly believes in freedom of expression and stands against censorship in all its forms. For more information, visit BooksBelong.com.
The Simon & Schuster Speakers Bureau can bring authors to your live event.
For more information or to book an event, contact the Simon & Schuster Speakers Bureau at 1-866-248-3049 or visit our website at www.simonspeakers.com.
Interior design by Rebecca Syracuse, Irene Metaxatos, and Hope Kim
The text for this book was set in Corundum Text Book.
The illustrations for this book were rendered digitally.
First Edition
10 9 8 7 6 5 4 3 2 1
Library of Congress Cataloging-in-Publication Data
Names: Cassidy, Taylor, author. | Bellet, Adriana.
Title: Black history is your history / Taylor Cassidy ; illustrated by Adriana Bellet.
Description: First edition. | New York : Atheneum Books for Young Readers, 2025. | Audience: Ages 12 up | Summary: "With sparkling wit and humor-and lots of fun pop culture references-digital content creator Taylor Cassidy (creator of TikTok sensation 'Fast Black History') takes readers on a journey through the Black history that she wishes she was taught in school. Weaving together research and personal anecdotes that illuminate each trailblazer's impact on her own life, Taylor paints a vibrant picture of twelve figures from Black history whose groundbreaking contributions shaped America as we know it today. From activists like Claudette Colvin and Marsha P. Johnson to literary giants Zora Neale Hurston and Maya Angelou, fashion designer Patrick Kelly, Olympic Gold medalist Tommie Smith, and more, this one-of-a-kind collection makes Black history relatable, relevant, and inspiring, so modern readers can recognize themselves within its pages. By the end, you'll want to proudly proclaim: 'Black history is my history!'"—Provided by publisher.
Identifiers: LCCN 2024035720 (print) | LCCN 2024035721 (ebook) | ISBN 9781665957700 (hardcover) | ISBN 9781665957724 (ebook)
Subjects: LCSH: African Americans—Biography—Juvenile literature. | African Americans—History—Juvenile literature. | Youth—Conduct of life—Juvenile literature.
Classification: LCC E185.96.C19 2025 (print) | LCC E185.96 (ebook) | DDC 920.009296073—dc23/eng/20241125
LC record available at https://lccn.loc.gov/2024035720
LC ebook record available at https://lccn.loc.gov/2024035721

FOR MY FAMILY AND FRIENDS,
WHOM I GIVE CREDIT FOR ALL THAT IS GOOD IN ME.

FOR TEACHERS AND EDUCATORS,
WHOSE EFFORT IS NEVER WASTED.

FOR FOREVER DREAMERS AND STUDENTS LIKE ME,
WHO DARE TO KEEP RISING.

CONTENTS
(AKA THE GPS OF THE BOOK)

INTRODUCTION 1

CLAUDETTE COLVIN
AND HOW TO MAKE CHANGE AT ANY AGE 7

BENJAMIN BANNEKER
AND HOW TO NEVER SHRINK YOURSELF 17

IDA B. WELLS
AND WHY TRUE STRENGTH MEANS BEING VULNERABLE 33

ZORA NEALE HURSTON
AND HOW TO EMBRACE YOUR COMPLEX IDENTITY 51

GORDON PARKS
AND WHEN IT'S TIME TO TAKE A RISK 65

LEDGER SMITH
AND HOW TO FIND CONFIDENCE IN NERVE-RACKING MOMENTS 81

TOMMIE SMITH
AND HOW TO KNOW WHO'S ON YOUR TEAM 93

CICELY TYSON
AND WHY GOOD REPRESENTATION CHANGES LIVES 109

MAYA ANGELOU
AND WHY YOUR ENERGY IS NEVER TOO MUCH 125

PATRICK KELLY
AND HOW REJECTION CAN BECOME REDIRECTION 139

MARSHA P. JOHNSON
AND WHY ANGER IS NOT AN ENEMY 159

MAE JEMISON
AND HOW DREAMING BIG WILL HELP YOU REACH THE STARS 173

ACKNOWLEDGMENTS 187

INTRODUCTION

HEY, READER!

My name is Taylor, and I am a Black history enthusiast. When some people say they really like a subject, they mean looking forward to a lecture about it in class. For me, I mean creating a viral TikTok web series teaching the Black history I've learned over the years to whoever would watch. As I'm writing this, that series (which I call *Fast Black History*) has earned me over two million followers.

In *Fast Black History*, I pull out all the tricks to visualize the story: wigs, green-screen effects, and the occasional fake mole when I'm dressed as Prince.

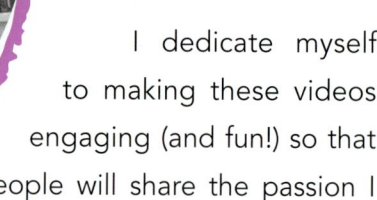

I dedicate myself to making these videos engaging (and fun!) so that people will share the passion I have for this topic. Since I started the series in 2020, I've received videos from real teachers who use *Fast Black History* videos as study tools in their classes, students who used them as motivation to start their own Black history clubs, and people who were inspired to create their own video series on different history topics. What I love most about Black history is that it doesn't feel stuck in the past. Every new thing I learn about an important figure in Black history influences my perspective on real decisions in my life. I am living proof that their impact is timeless.

I started on this path early. My parents thought it was crucial for my sister and me to learn Black history growing up. My childhood was filled with random pop quizzes in the car about the civil rights movement and movie nights watching *Roots* (every now and then I still get Quincy Jones's soundtrack for the show stuck in my head).

I remember feeling more eager to watch movies about Black history than to read about it in books. The reason wasn't just because I thought the dress of the girl who acted as Ruby Bridges was stylish, but also because when I'd pick up the Black history biographies my mother bought for us, I'd find intimidating pages filled with tiny words and no pictures at all. (*No pictures?* Collective eleven-year-old gasp!) This was not appealing to a tween who only read books if they had a pretty cover and held her interest for more than five minutes. If your summer reading book didn't look like the middle-school equivalent of a luxury purse, what was the point in reading it?

Instead of books, most of the education on Black history I got growing up was from my parents' stories and from my teachers spending about fifteen minutes every February lecturing the same unit about Martin Luther King Jr. and Rosa Parks. Don't get me wrong, learning about Rosa Parks is like watching a good rerun of your favorite show: it impacts you every time. But there was always a missing piece in my learning. I lacked interactivity and connection. I wish I'd had a book that truly connected Black history to *my* life experience and showed me that the courage, creativity, and perseverance that drove Black historical figures were things I could also find in myself. I needed an author to take me on a journey with them—a tour through the *world* of Black contributions that my school curriculum overlooked—where they'd show me how interesting (and cool!) Black history can be. Maybe, reader, you've been wanting a book like that too.

So boom. I got the solution. *This* book!

I'll take you through the exciting stories of twelve Black American historical figures. Don't worry, y'all, this is *not* a history textbook. Fair warning and disclaimer: I may not have a history diploma, but I do have *charisma*, which is just as credible! (Don't fact-check that.) In each chapter, I'll be adding a little creative interpretation on how I imagine that historical figure would think or react to the real situations they were in—and that imaginary version of them might use some pretty modern language! But I'll never tell you history that isn't true. You'll always know what is fact and what is from my imagination.

In addition to these figures' narratives, I'll also tell you stories from my past and the life lessons ya girl learned from them. These Black history figures and I have some triumphant, funny, and slightly embarrassing (okay, *very* embarrassing) moments to share with you. Not only will I prepare you with the knowledge to impress your crush in fourth-period history class, but you'll also discover how the ambitions and personal thoughts of these historical figures aren't much different from mine, or from your own. As you read, you'll see yourself in history and realize that you also have the power to change the world, just as the people in this book did. (Heck yeah!)

While this book is in no way a substitute for better Black

history education in schools, I hope it jump-starts your own curiosity to learn more. And after you finish the last page, I hope you can proudly say, "Black history is *my* history!"

PS: If you ever question how long I've loved telling stories from Black history, first-grade Taylor reading a Rosa Parks book to her class has the receipts.

And, yes, I would in fact still rock a hot pink leopard-print jacket and matching pants like I did in this photo.

CLAUDETTE COLVIN
AND HOW TO MAKE CHANGE AT ANY AGE

CONGRATULATIONS! YOU'VE MADE IT TO THE FIRST chapter of my book! Now I have a question for you. Do you know who Rosa Parks is? The woman who refused to give up her seat on a segregated bus in 1955, effectively sparking one of the first big events in the civil rights movement?

You do know her? Great.

Well, surprise! This first story isn't about her. It's about a girl named Claudette Colvin, who also refused to give up her seat. But here's the kicker: Claudette did it nine months *before* Rosa did, and she was only fifteen at the time. *Dramatic gasp!*

After a plot twist like that, you might be wondering why

we hear so much about Rosa Parks but not Claudette Colvin. I mean, Claudette was just a high schooler! And even though she was young, she was ready to defend her humanity. How awesome is that? However, even though the NAACP supported Claudette, they chose to make Rosa the face of the bus boycott—and thus, the face of the growing civil rights movement—instead. Rosa Parks was older than Claudette and had lighter skin, which made her more appealing to the public. In an interview with the *New York Times,* Claudette recalled her mother warning her to "be quiet about what I did. She told me, 'Let Rosa be the one. White people aren't going to bother Rosa—her skin is lighter than yours and they like her.'"

Are you telling me Claudette's actions were for nothing? That's crazy!

Luckily, "useless" is the last word you'd use to describe Claudette's bravery. While Claudette's name hasn't resounded through civil rights history as loudly as it should have, her decision to challenge laws that day was instrumental in fighting for desegregation on buses.

I'll set the scene for you. In Montgomery, Alabama, in March of 1955, Claudette had just finished another day at high school. On her way home with her classmates, she thought about all she had learned recently. Last month had been Negro History Month at school, which meant the teachers' lessons had focused on the many people who contributed to Claudette's present quality of life.

As she walked, her thoughts weren't only on figures like

Sojourner Truth and W. E. B. Du Bois, but also on the conversations she and her classmates had had about the ongoing struggles Black people faced. I can imagine her hugging her schoolbooks to her chest as she walked to the bus stop, thinking about whether segregation would forever ban people who looked like her from doing things like sitting at a lunch counter to be served their favorite coffee or trying on the newest pair of Mary Janes at the shoe shop on the corner. When I first learned about Claudette as a teenager, I realized she might have had the same worries I did at her age. ("What outfit will I wear to school tomorrow? Does Willie from math class like me?") However, like many Black teenagers during that time, she also carried the burden of inequality on top of those worries.

TAYSTORY!

Whoa, what is this?

Well, dear reader, this is TAYSTORY! Get it? History + Taylor. Throughout this book I'll be sharing parts of my life that show how each Black history figure we're learning about has affected and inspired me personally. This way you'll see even more deeply why Black history matters, how it's helped me reach for my dreams, and how it can inspire you, too.

My junior year of high school, I decided to take Advanced Placement US History. Yes, it would look better on my college application, but what I really hoped for was a deeper understanding and knowledge of Black American history. When I was growing up, the only time I learned the history of my own people in school was during Black History Month every February. It was like how Michael Bublé only pops up during Christmastime to sing "Jingle Bells" and then seems to disappear come New Year's. And every year, we only learned about the same three or four figures (shout-out to Rosa Parks, Martin Luther King Jr., and Frederick Douglass). While I appreciated getting to watch movies about these people instead of practicing long division, I started to realize over the years that the amount of history I'd learned about White people was vastly greater than that of Black people. I started to think, *There should be more about Black people in this textbook. It's a desert out here! Where are my people?* So, when I signed up for this AP history course in high school, I hoped the challenging academics it promised meant the inclusion of more diversity.

What I got was definitely academic and had a whole lot of challenges, but not in the way I expected. Because I attended a school with minimal people of color, most of my classmates were White. Now, there's nothing wrong with being White, but many of them didn't have the same awareness I did of the gaps in the history that we had all learned, or the same inclination to question what they'd heard. I slowly started noticing ignorant comments from my classmates during every lesson about Black  people, slavery, and the civil rights movement. Listen, man, these were the kind of comments that would make Harriet Tubman roll in her grave—and they certainly made it hard to sit through class. Every day, I would leave my history lessons with a burning in my chest. One that made me feel like if I didn't do or say something, the fire inside me would gobble me up whole.

On the first day of February, I was feeling this burning again. It was the first day of Black History Month, and I knew in my heart that it was the perfect time to take action. Sitting on my bedroom floor, I thought about all the Black history I had learned, mostly from my parents. I thought about the platform I had on TikTok, where I had just hit one hundred thousand followers a few days before (on my birthday! Yes, it was the best birthday gift).

I set up my phone and filmed a fifteen-second clip about an influential Black chemist named Percy Julian. I titled the video "Fast Black History."

Even before posting it, I knew this was the beginning of a series I had to continue. It felt like my desire to understand more about all the figures I'd learned about growing up had manifested itself into something I could share with my followers. I thought, *Even if no one watches the video, I'll be proud that I did something. I'll be content knowing that I did my best to teach Black history the way I wish someone had taught me.* Unaware of just how much this series would change my life, I hit the "post" button.

More than ten thousand people liked the TikTok in a week. Needless to say, I was stunned! I kept educating, and by the end of April one million people had hit the "follow" button—and many more had viewed my videos. I was delighted by all the people who enjoyed learning Black history, and I loved hearing how it comforted them as they faced challenges in their own lives. I realized I felt the same way as a lot of my TikTok viewers: each time I looked back on my own story, I noticed how often I'd had the same feelings of anxiety, hope, and courage as the Black history figures I taught about, and how much learning their stories motivated me to overcome obstacles in my own life.

That's why I'm telling you about Claudette Colvin. If you're like me and have ever felt the urge to stand up for yourself or take action against something you know isn't right, you'll understand how Claudette felt in her story.

When the bus arrived, Claudette paid her fare and took a seat. Thoughts of hope, and the ways she might help the progress for equality, filled her mind as she looked out the window onto the busy rush-hour street.

Suddenly, Claudette heard a voice above her. When she looked up, she saw a White woman and the bus driver sternly staring at her.

"You got to get up!" the bus driver said.

Oh, he means business. Claudette assessed the situation. The bus was busy that day, and that woman seemed to want to sit in her seat.

But, Taylor, why couldn't homegirl just stand if there were no seats left?

The issue was, if this White woman stood while Claudette had a comfortable seat, it would have meant she had no power over Claudette. It would have shown they were equal. The woman would have rather moved someone else from their seat than be looked at as equal to a Black person. Now, if I were Claudette, I would've told the woman off and given the bus driver a wedgie.

No, you wouldn't have.

Correct, reader. No, I wouldn't have. I can't fight. But luckily,

Claudette knew another way to stand (or sit) her ground.

As Claudette processed these two people yelling for her to move from her seat, she recognized the ridiculousness in all of it. She had paid the same fare and chosen her seat just like everyone else. Why should she get up just because another person was made uncomfortable by her existence?

So she sat and didn't move. You know that burning that I felt in my history class? Claudette must have felt the same thing, because she was quoted in *Newsweek* saying, "I felt like Sojourner Truth was pushing down on one shoulder and Harriet Tubman was pushing down on the other—saying, 'Sit down, girl!'" Though this act would lead to her being arrested, charged for violating segregation laws, and placed in jail, it got the NAACP's attention, and they later planned a bus boycott that would change the entire nation.

Rosa Parks, who was already a part of the local NAACP chapter, had been following along and supporting Claudette's case. She even helped Claudette attend local NAACP Youth meetings to tell her story. So when Rosa refused to give up her seat months later, she no doubt had Claudette Colvin in her heart. When the issue of bus segregation was brought to the Supreme Court, Claudette was a plaintiff along with three other women—and the plaintiffs won. The Supreme Court declared segregation on buses unconstitutional, a major victory in the decades-long fight for civil rights in the United States.

Reader, never believe there's an age requirement to do good. Claudette didn't think, *I'm not allowed to spark change because I'm too young.* She felt inspired by the victories of those who came before her, and when it was time to make history herself, she learned that a world-changing legacy can be started at any age and last forever.

BENJAMIN BANNEKER
AND HOW TO NEVER SHRINK YOURSELF

BENJAMIN BANNEKER WAS LIKE SPIDER-MAN. That's right. One day in colonial times, when he was a kid, a mysterious colonial bug crawled out of his colonial teacup and bit him on his colonial arm. All of a sudden, he could shoot colonial spiderwebs! But unfortunately, because there were no green goblins and skyscrapers hadn't been invented yet, all he could really do with his powers was glue the soles on his colonial shoes back together . . . colonially.

Thanks for reading! Make sure to follow, like, and subscribe on my social media!

Just kidding. Benjamin Banneker did not shoot spiderwebs like Peter Parker, *but* they did have a couple of things in common: having alliterative first and last names . . . and more importantly, being science PRODIGIES. As a kid, Benjamin spent his days falling in love with the study of math, astrology, and writing. Not much is known about his early life, but most historians agree that he had only a brief formal education from a Quaker school near his home. The real fun would come when he used his *own* research to create some pretty amazing things.

Have you ever taken apart a radio or your mom's sewing machine to see how all the parts fit together? If you have, you've also probably had to take on double chores for a week after realizing you couldn't put it back together (sorry, Mom!). But Benjamin could take things apart *and* put them back together—and studying gadgets was only the starting point for his creativity. When he was twenty-one, he looked at a pocket watch one day and thought, *Oh, that's light work,* and hand-made an entire clock that could chime accurately on the hour. On top of that, he did it with no instructions—just his own math calculations and *vibes*. I'm always impressed by this because if someone told me to build a wardrobe from IKEA without the manual, I'd accidentally build a door to bootleg Narnia. So yeah, Benjamin and his clock became the *tock* of the town. (I could make so many more clockwork puns, but I don't want to *grind your gears*.) People visited Ben's farm just to get a look at his creation and would be delighted at its chime.

Okay, Taylor, big deal. He made a clock. I have, like, four of them in my house right now. How hard could it be?

Well, dear reader, at this time there weren't many American-made wooden mechanical clocks in existence. On top of that, Benjamin Banneker's is widely believed to have been one of the first ones made in the thirteen colonies. It's like if your best friend showed up to school with homemade virtual reality goggles.

If you've learned about American colonial history from your social studies class, you might be wondering something. How could Benjamin read, write, and go to school if this was all happening before slavery was abolished?

He was able to do all that because his parents were *freemen*. His father, formerly enslaved, had earned enough money to buy his freedom before Benjamin was born. But although Benjamin's parents owned land, lived outside of slavery, and ran their own farming business, freemen were still considered inferior because their skin color was seen as something unfortunate and unworthy. For Benjamin, those must have been heavy social burdens to carry, especially when he was born with a love of education—something commonly withheld at the time from people who looked like him.

But he also would have known some things that refuted every negative stereotype. I can imagine Benjamin listening to his father tell stories of Africa, where he'd been born. Benjamin must have reveled in knowing that outside the colonies, Black people owned businesses, led their own communities, and even ruled empires. If I had been Benjamin during that time, knowing what Black people could accomplish would have strengthened my self-worth and reminded me that the opinions of people around me could never define my value or ability.

Benjamin soon took over his family's farm, running their crop business and designing his very own irrigation system.

What the heck is an irrigation system?

I'm glad you asked! Without any prior Googling and *totally* just knowing this knowledge off the top of my head, let me tell you! Our Benny boy created the equivalent of a sprinkler system so that all his family's crops would be watered automatically. He did this by digging strategically placed trenches to direct water from the creek on their land straight toward the crops. This irrigation system worked so well, Benjamin's plants even thrived during *droughts*. SPIDER-MAN SCIENCE PRODIGY THINGS!

And his community knew he was a Spider-Man science prodigy! He was well-known in his area for being a successful businessman. Once the Ellicotts, a wealthy family from Pennsylvania, bought land near Benjamin's, they quickly caught on to his intense intellect. What started as exchanging books on astrology and science turned into Andrew Ellicott hiring Benjamin Banneker to be part of the team that would design the street layout for . . . wait for it . . .

The Nation's Capital.

The Revolutionary War was over, and Congress had decided to build a city on the Potomac River to be the new nation's capital. Benjamin used his incredible mind for astronomical calculations that helped determine the city's boundaries. This was an essential part of forming the nation's lawmaking and governmental grounds—aka a *big deal*! Being on that team should have served as a direct rebuttal against common beliefs that Black people were inferior and unable to think critically. However, in historical documents, Benjamin's work was credited to Andrew Ellicott. Benjamin wasn't even mentioned!

Hadn't the United States written in its Declaration of Independence that "all men are created equal"? So why was Benjamin still being treated like he was worth nothing?

When Benjamin read the paper, he'd still find articles talking nonsense about Africans, like one written by the *very same* man who had authored the Declaration of Independence, Thomas Jefferson. Here's something Jefferson wrote about people of African descent in *Notes on the State of Virginia* in 1785: "They seem to require less sleep. A black, after hard labour through the day, will be induced by the slightest amusements to sit up till midnight, or later, though knowing he must be out with the first dawn of the morning."

This man was really confused about why everybody didn't have a wittle-bitty bedtime like him! Aww! What I imagine was *really* going on was the people he enslaved spilling tea about him in private during the only communal free time they had.

Benjamin knew that he was intellectual, wise, and incredibly qualified to receive the same amount of recognition and acknowledgment as his White counterparts. But it must have been discouraging to know his worth and still have it be ignored by others.

TAYSTORY!

Have y'all ever been to the zoo and visited the butterfly room? It's magical. You're surrounded by colorful butterflies that are constantly fluttering from one place to another. It looks like confetti and flower petals flying through the air. That feeling, the feeling I had standing in my local zoo's butterfly exhibit, is the same way I felt when I looked at my pookie wookie bookie boo bear crush in high school. He was *my man*, okay? He just . . . didn't know it.

Every morning I would sit impatiently in my first class of the day, counting down the minutes until our time together. Once it was time for French, I would straighten my back, check my appearance in the bathroom mirror, and waltz in like the mysterious, nonchalant teen I aspired to be. For his part, he looked like a normal high school boy, but he was also the *foreign exchange student*. Cue the *ooooohs* and *ahhhhs*. To high school me, the fact that he spoke multiple languages, knew what life was like outside the Midwest, and had freckles (freckles!) was all that was required to set my sights on him.

And y'all . . . I did more than just crush on him. I. Did.

The. Most. I made it a point to walk him to his class every day, made sure he was on my team for every group project, sent him daily updates on Snapchat, the whole thing. I even offered to drive this boy to school 'cause he didn't have a ride!

No! Taylor! Not the gas money!

I know, reader, I know. But you couldn't tell me anything back then. In my head, every effort was simply me proving my worth to him as a potential romantic partner.

But something started to shift as the weeks went by. I started realizing that the butterflies in my stomach felt less like confetti and more like fear. All of a sudden I felt unbearably self-conscious. *Does my hair look too poofy today? I think I'm crossing my legs wrong. Don't make that face; he'll think you're weird. Try harder to talk to him tomorrow; you're not doing enough.* To make matters worse, my French teacher saw how much I talked to him and assigned us seats *right* next to each other in the very front of the room. I was so overcome with nerves that I'd race to class each day so I could arrive before him and not have to squeeze into my seat with him watching me.

My pookie wookie shmookie boo didn't feel as fun to crush on anymore, because every time I saw him, I made myself feel small. On top of that, he rarely responded to my texts, never looked me in the eye, and only talked to me when his friends weren't in class that day—or when he wanted answers to our French homework.

Now, what I *should* have said to him was "Tu ne me mérites pas! / You don't deserve me!", but instead, I grew more and more insecure. I continued waiting by my phone for his texts, being extra careful about what outfits I wore, and creating plans to win him over. I was *infatuated* and didn't know how to let go. I even remember talking about him to my mom, and I was just as baffled as her when I heard myself say, "I feel so small in his presence!"

Pause. Homegirl, you talk about this lil boy like he has god status!

I had a big realization of how low I'd set the bar for myself and an even more humiliating one about the lengths I'd go to stoop down to that bar. I wish I could say I stopped crushing on him right then and there, but to Megan Thee Stallion's dismay, I did in fact stand and wait outside for this man on our last day of class so I could ask him out. He said yes—but then ghosted me for the rest of the summer.

To be frank, I knew I was poppin'! I believed I was beautiful, funny, and that if "I Like It" by Cardi B came on at homecoming, I could dance *circles* around you! But the more I felt rejected by someone who didn't see my worth, the more I thought the answer was shrinking myself to become more digestible for *him*. At the time, I was afraid of losing my crush as a potential love interest because that would have seemed like proof that I didn't deserve love at all.

Reader, you deserve more than to beg for someone's approval. Listen when I say that you are worthy *without* having to prove it to anyone else. If they are not excited about *all* your spirit, walk away.

As summer ended and crushy wushy pie bear went back to his home country, my emotions lessened and my heart moved on. I learned that pulling your energy away from relationships and friends that aren't supportive isn't "giving up" or "being mean." It's self-love. Moreover, I forgave myself for not knowing better and promised to never shame myself again for the heartfelt way I express love or care for someone; instead, I'd pour it into the people in my life who *did* see my worth. No shrinking necessary.

Many times, staying quiet and shrinking ourselves into a shape that we think other people might like better feels like the easier option. You and I will never face the intense experience of living as a Black man in the 1700s, like Benjamin Banneker did, but we can *all* relate to the feeling of being underestimated and overlooked in our daily lives and being tempted to keep ourselves as small as others make us feel. But Benjamin Banneker made the riskier decision to stand up for his worth—in a *huge* way. I hope hearing the rest of his story will inspire you to do the same in your own life.

Do you think if I wrote a colonial Spider-Man comic, they'd include it in the Spider-Verse franchise? No? Well, if I were alive in the 1700s, I could just publish it in my own almanac instead!

Taylor, what's an almanac? I'm gonna need you to Google that, too.

An almanac was like if you took the weather app on your phone and combined it with your daily horoscope. It was a book that predicted the moon phases and the weather and provided farming and gardening advice. If the author of the almanac liked having fun, they'd also throw in their own thoughts about the world, politics, and more! These babies sold like hotcakes back in the day. Almanacs were many households' essential guides to planting crops, managing land, and predicting their profits. By purchasing an almanac, you were basically entrusting the author with the outcome of your harvest and aligning yourself with their opinions about the world.

With science and politics on the forefront of Benjamin Banneker's mind, the almanac industry was right up his alley—so he decided to write one. All the expertise and skills he'd worked hard to build over his lifetime went into this almanac. He used his own calculations to measure constellations and predict the season's forecast, and he shared his tips for better gardening. And of course, he casually threw in a major diss to Thomas Jefferson, who was the secretary of state at the time. The almanac included a letter to Jefferson about his hypocrisy in the Declaration of Independence—and Benjamin was so eager to make his case that, before the almanac was published, he handwrote an entire advance copy to send directly to Jefferson.

Please pull out your colonial reading glasses! It's time to read some snippets of Benjamin's letter. Don't worry! Because we're talking the 1700s and I grew up with my sister, who was and is still a musical theater nerd, I've taken the liberty of translating the letter to modern language in my best attempt at a *Hamilton*-style historical rap. TAYLORZANDER HAMILTAY!

> *"Sir, I freely and cheerfully acknowledge, that I am of the African race, and in that colour which is natural to them of the deepest dye; and it is under a sense of the most profound gratitude to the Supreme Ruler of the Universe, that I now confess to you, that I am not under that state of tyrannical thraldom, and inhuman captivity, to which too many of my brethren are doomed . . .*

> *They say the blacker the berry,*
> *the sweeter the juice;*
> *Well, get ready to harvest,*
> *'cause I'm in full bloom.*
> *I'm livin' without chains*
> *'cause of my mama and daddy,*
> *But if I could, I'd free all my brothers gladly.*
> *That means my melanin ain't stopping me from*
> *sippin' from the same tea*
> *And writing letters proudly to you, lil Tommy.*
> *And while I have you here*
> *let's refresh your memory.*
> *My name is Big Ben.*
> *This is your bedtime story.*

"This, Sir, was a time when you clearly saw into the injustice of a state of slavery, and in which you had just apprehensions of the horrors of its condition. It was now that your abhorrence thereof was so excited, that you publicly held forth this true and invaluable doctrine, which is worthy to be recorded and remembered in all succeeding ages: 'We hold these truths to be self-evident, that all men are created equal...'"

> Ain't you the one who said slavery was wrong?
> Maybe you forgot once your British friends were gone.
> I'll lend you my intelligence since yours is asleep
> I planned cities in your nation while you counted sheep.

"... but, Sir, how pitiable is it to reflect, that although you were so fully convinced of the benevolence of the Father of Mankind, and of his equal and impartial distribution of these rights and privileges, which he hath conferred upon them, that you should at the same time counteract his mercies, in detaining by fraud and violence so numerous a part of my brethren, under groaning captivity and cruel oppression, that you should at the same time be found guilty of that most criminal act, which you professedly detested in others, with respect to yourselves."

> *"All men created equal," yada yada, you know the rest.*
> *You're acting like a child cheating moves while playing chess.*
> *I tried to put it kindly but here's the ugly fact:*
> *Your thoughts on slavery are like a pot calling the kettle black.*
> *Are contradictions a hobby you take pleasure in?*
> *You'll love this; here's your thoughts on Africans:*
> *"Inferior in the body and the mind."*
> *But who built your cities while you sat back and reclined?*
> *You looked loud, limp, and lazy as you overlooked my mind.*
> *My calculations were smoother than the clock I made chime.*
> *In your own words y'all's beauty is "superior,"*
> *But that powdered wig is stiff and your eye bags look drearier.*

OOOOHHHH!!!! HE ATE HIM UP!!!!

Okay, Benjamin Banneker didn't insult any powdered wigs in his letter, but he made Jefferson's hypocrisy incredibly clear and didn't spare Lil Tommy's feelings.

How did Jefferson respond to the letter? He said thanks for the almanac and expressed his hopes that the systems in America could change to help improve the "condition" of Black people's minds "to what it ought to be." He said he'd send the almanac to the Academy of Sciences in France to prove Benjamin's intelligence, despite his being Black.

Benjamin Banneker often received this kind of response to his work. Instead of seeing his intellect as evidence that stereotypes about Black people were wrong, people often described Benjamin as a wonder or marvel, as if he'd overcome some kind of hindrance to be so intelligent—the hindrance being his skin color.

Benjamin could have hidden his skills and presented a more palatable version of himself for others, but instead, he fought for what he deserved. His almanac was published in 1792, and his correspondence with Thomas Jefferson was later circulated in various other publications and used in many abolitionist efforts. For the rest of his life, Benjamin kept publishing more works and never stopped learning. Meanwhile, prejudiced people never stopped looking down on him.

When he passed away in 1806, most of Benjamin's work and writings were burned in a mysterious fire that destroyed his home on the day of his funeral. In a last attempt to conceal any evidence of Benjamin's success and status, someone turned to a devastating act, ruining the life's work of a great mind. But what that fire couldn't destroy was the lasting impression Benjamin had made on everyone around him. His neighbors, the Ellicotts, passionately recounted the life of Benjamin Banneker in multiple biographies and kept a record of his work alive for us to know about today. This goes to show that when you aren't afraid to speak up for your value, others will be inspired by your passion and join you.

Banneker lived as a Black man who was publicly against slavery in a time when that could put you in real danger. His outspokenness and contributions to early civil rights advocacy spoke volumes about his bravery. If Benjamin Banneker had the security and peace in himself to stand up to someone as powerful as Thomas Jefferson, then I know *I* can also make moves, big or small, to ensure I'm living honestly and to my fullest potential—no matter what expectation is thrown at me.

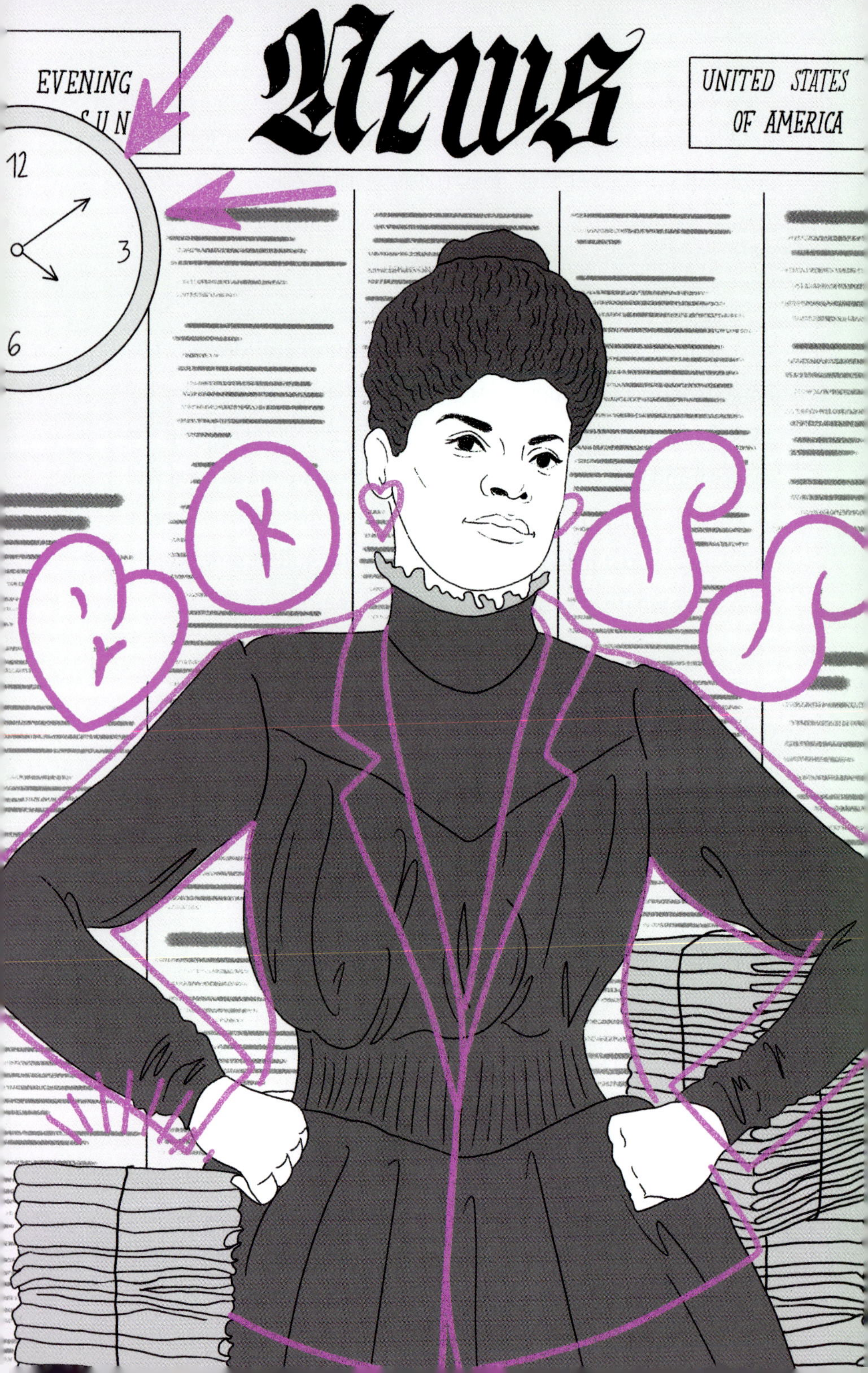

EVENING SUN
News
UNITED STATES OF AMERICA
12
3
6

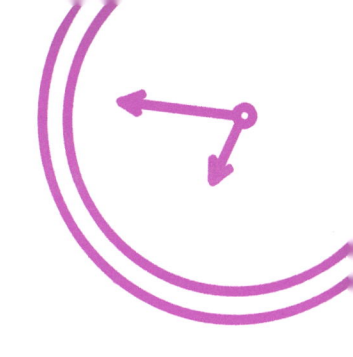

IDA B. WELLS
AND WHY TRUE STRENGTH MEANS BEING VULNERABLE

WAIT!

> This chapter includes discussion of Black trauma and violence. Read at your own risk—or if you need to, go ahead and skip this chapter. No hard feelings! We all must protect our joy sometimes.

HAVE YOU EVER SEEN SOMEONE DESCRIBED AS A "Strong Black Woman"? If you're wondering where the label came from, it can be connected to the suffering Black women have historically faced: during slavery, the civil rights movement, and even today. A person who has never experienced racism or prejudice might look at someone who has and assume that simply because they have survived it, they are less affected by it. But that kind of thinking ends up hurting people.

To show why, let me tell you something wild! Some researchers from the University of Virginia did a scientific study in 2016, published in *Proceedings of the National Academy of Sciences of the United States of America*, where they gave surveys to both medical students and people without medical education. They showed people statements like "Blacks age more slowly than Whites" and "Black people's skin is thicker than White people's skin" and asked them to say whether they were true or false. The goal was to see if people still thought there were significant biological differences in Black people. In the end, many participants showed that they thought Black patients had the ability to experience less pain than White patients—including about *half* of the medical students surveyed.

That study shows that there are probably people currently working in hospitals and doctors' offices who think Black people somehow experience diseases and ailments with less suffering! Everyone, I *promise you* that if Black people were somehow born with the ability to turn off pain receptors like a light switch, ya girl would have had *way* fewer fights with my mom about detangling my hair. (If I see a rattail comb on the street? We're squaring up 'cause I still have beef.)

Imagine waking up with a really bad toothache. It's so bad your jaw is sore to the touch, so you visit the dentist. Then, this dentist assumes you feel less pain than them based on what you look like. As you're describing the ache to them, they respond with "You seem fine to me! You're overreacting." You'd probably feel pretty upset. And you might feel a lot more hesitant to tell someone about your worries the next time—which means you don't get the care you need.

The "Strong Black Woman" stereotype doesn't only affect healthcare for physical problems. It can prevent Black women from finding safe spaces where they can be vulnerable and express their feelings, affecting their mental health, too.

Every time I read about Ida B. Wells, I feel she is defined by the "Strong Black Woman" label. She's usually described as fearless, brave, and endlessly tough. However, I think when she's only talked about in this way, her character and humanity fall flat. I seek to see her depth. When I think about her, I am astonished not *only* by her resilience but also by her ability to be publicly vulnerable, let her guard down, and freely express every emotion in her heart. I'm someone who grew up finding it hard to tell even my closest friends about my pains, thinking I had to fight alone, so learning about Ida B. Wells changed my narrative about what true strength looks like.

Ida B. Wells was born about five months before Abraham Lincoln signed the Emancipation Proclamation, which freed enslaved people in Confederate states and became a stepping-stone to the eventual outlawing of slavery in the United States. She grew up in a postwar era when Black people were surrounded by new possibilities. For many, this was a chance to build their own lives from the ground up. Even though systemic injustices like Black codes, segregation, and straight-up hate crimes were common, entrepreneurship in the Black community still blossomed.

It was go-go-go mode for many in this era, and the same

can be said for Ida. In her adolescent years, her parents and one of her six siblings passed away due to yellow fever, leaving Ida responsible for taking care of the rest of the family. She worked as a teacher to make ends meet, and reading and education became her escape from grief. She decided to attend Fisk University, one of the earliest historically Black colleges in the US. In addition to teaching students and attending school, Ida wrote for a weekly paper under the pen name "Iola," sharing her unfiltered emotions and thoughts on segregation, racism, and feminism. One of her notable publications, which sparked national attention, chronicled her experience being dragged off a train after refusing to change cars because of her race.

Ida was *on it*. From the start, her drive to build a better life for herself and her family was clear. She was the kind of person who took action by being straightforward—and, if necessary, blunt—in her words and opinions when something needed to be changed. In other words, if Ida B. Wells were at your school and you decided to pair fuzzy green polka-dot bell-bottoms with a neon-orange basketball jersey on picture day, Ida would *not* hold back in saying how crazy you looked.

After she established a reputation for her journalism, Ida found an opportunity to take her writing to the next level. *New character alert!* Enter Reverend Taylor Nightingale. This man was the pastor of a church in Memphis. But oh, this wasn't just any church. It was one of the largest in Tennessee. So you can imagine that when he opened a newspaper with his business partner, J. L. Fleming, it flew off shelves at every Sunday service. The *Memphis Free Speech and Headlight* caught a glimpse of Ida's writings and invited her to join the paper.

Before she said yes, she had a specific requirement. She decided that if she worked for the *Memphis Free Speech and Headlight*, she must be considered one of the owners of the newspaper—so she bought a third of it and became a shareholder. By becoming the editor of the *Memphis Free Speech and Headlight*, Ida had much more creative control over what she wrote, how she wrote, and how often she could write about it.

In Ida's articles for the *Memphis Free Speech and Headlight*, she laid out all the details of the poor education given to African American children in the school district where she worked. She exposed the immoral teachers and deficient school buildings. Sugarcoating was not Ida's style, so her words got a *lot* of eyes. After the Memphis school board saw her articles, Ida was fired from her teaching position.

Ida lost the job that fed her family and kept a roof over their heads because of her writing. It would have been understandable if she'd decided to stop publishing articles. But writing was one of the only places Ida could go and feel no limits. All her responsibilities, and all the pressure to keep up in a world built against Black women with an opinion, didn't matter so long as she held a pen. Writing was a *necessity* for Ida—the thing that brought her life purpose and fulfillment, offered an escape from the world and an outlet for her energy and creativity, and made her want to be a better person. In her autobiography, Ida said that when she wrote, she could "express the real 'me'" and that she "enjoyed [her] work to the utmost."

Heck yeah! Ida B. Wells was using her voice for good! With the addition of her daring writing, the *Memphis Free Speech and Headlight* was *boomin'*. If you wanted tea about the town, this newspaper was where it was *at*. And if you couldn't read very well, no problem. Ida made sure to write in a plain, understandable way that was accessible to everyone. To make the newspaper even trendier, it was printed on *pink paper*. Nine-year-old Taylor would have been *obsessed*.

The *Memphis Free Speech and Headlight* didn't tiptoe around the truth. Its articles criticized politicians who worked against the rights of Black people, church members who took advantage of their position, and even nationally known public figure Booker T. Washington, for sharing how uneducated he believed Black pastors were with a White newspaper.

Ida loved her work, and so did the Black community. The success of the paper raised Ida's salary to almost as much as she'd made as a teacher and took her from city to city to speak at meetings and conventions. Ida described being "treated like a queen" during those excursions. The kind of life Ida had—where she was able to write her own newspaper, own a business, live off her passion, and speak out against injustice all while being a Black woman—was not common in those days. She was rare and special in many people's eyes. Life felt good and Ida felt purposeful as she traveled the country—but disaster was happening back home.

Thomas Moss, or "Tommie," was one of Ida's best friends in Memphis. They were so close that Ida was the godmother to his child and friends with his entire family. Ida admired Tommie for his passion and similar values of correcting wrongs swiftly. I can imagine Tommie and Ida sitting on the front porch for hours, talking about a book she'd just finished and joking about how she should have brought him back a souvenir from her last work trip.

Tommie was as driven and focused as Ida. He opened his own grocery store called the People's Grocery with two other men, Will Stewart and Calvin McDowell, in a heavily Black part of town, and soon had a successful business. Although his store competed with a White man's, Tommie personally knew many people in town and was sure his shop would be supported. Still, he was taking a risk. This was a time of many new entrepreneurial efforts made by Black people—but lots of White people despised Black-owned businesses. The more Black people openly embraced their freedom, the more their lives and well-being were threatened. It was extremely common for Black lives and establishments to be put in danger for little reason. Sometimes, as a Black person, all it took was one wrong glance at a White person, or a smart word spoken at the wrong moment, to make you a target. In Tommie's case, it was a marbles game.

A group of Black and White boys playing with marbles near Tommie's store got into a fight. This led to an adult White man attacking one of the Black boys and Tommie's co-owners from the People's Grocery stepping in to stop him. When police got involved, Tommie's business was blamed for the entire incident. White people in the area threatened to pay a not-so-peaceful visit to his grocery store. They came at closing time but were met by armed men protecting the store. Shots rang out and several White men were wounded. Local police pounced on this, raiding homes in the neighborhood and arresting dozens of Black men whom they deemed suspicious; one of these men was Tommie Moss. A few days later, a mob of White people stormed the jail, dragged Tommie and his grocery store co-owners out of their cells, drove them outside city limits, and lynched them. Over a petty game of marbles, Ida's best friend's life was taken horribly and abruptly. Soon after, Tommie's store was raided and shut down, making it obvious that the real motivation behind his murder was to get rid of his Black-owned business.

Ida returned from a business trip to find her friend already buried. This was a person Ida laughed with, confided in, and most likely came to for support and advice. His was the friendly face she passed on the street during her lunch break. His smile was a reminder of friendship, family, and comfort. Now she would never see it again. Instead, Ida saw newspapers justifying Tommie's and the other men's deaths by calling them criminals who took advantage of women. These papers painted the murderers as heroes protecting the morality of the town.

This event drove Ida to visit places where other lynchings happened, to interview the victims' families and communities and uncover the truths that *other* newspapers weren't telling. She discovered brutal acts, outright manipulation, and blatant lies that covered up the true crimes of murdering Black people. Ida printed these findings in pamphlets that heavily criticized the lynchings, not only in Memphis but all over the South. She contradicted newspapers that painted lynchings as chivalrous by revealing the innocence of their victims. She also emphasized in her writing how different life could be for Black people outside Memphis, causing more and more families to move away.

Wow, Ida must have been so fearless and strong!

Yes, she was, but all this still must have been extremely hard on her. She must have had days when all she wanted was to slam a big wall between her and the world to protect her weakened, grieving heart. She published her first pamphlet about lynchings barely seven months after her closest friend passed away, and in her writing she opened up her heart and soul for all to see. I can't imagine the pain Ida went through, reliving the trauma of her friend's death over and over for the sake of spreading truth.

What did she receive in return? While she was on a trip to New York, a White mob ransacked the *Free Speech* office and destroyed everything. Learning of this in the morning paper, Ida read that they'd also threatened to give her the same fate as her friend should she ever return to Memphis. In an instant, Ida was estranged from her business, her home, and her community. She lost it all. She'd poured out her everything for *Free Speech*, and bigotry took it all away.

TAYSTORY!

If someone asked me to describe myself using a celebrity quote, I'd have to throw on a honey-brown lace front and recite Beyoncé to them: "I don't like to gamble, but if there is one thing I'm willing to bet on, it's myself." Spontaneously picking up new hobbies and *mastering* them is like a game for me. Cheerleading, photography, and intricate nail art are just a few activities I decided to become an expert in at some point. I treat weeks-long projects like *life or death*, okay? Here's a top three list of my most niche projects:

1. **Snack Wrappers on the Floor:** A parody YouTube video of Bruno Mars's hit song "Versace on the Floor." This three-week-long, two-location production enlisted my friends as backup dancers, had costumes sourced from old show-choir outfits, and featured lyrics (recorded by my sister) about preferring to spend a night in eating pizza and watching Netflix over partying with friends. Here's the

first chorus: "Snack wrappers on the floor. Ooh! My friends party without me. I just like eating more. Doesn't mean that I'm lonely, yeah." The MTV Video Music Awards lost my submission in the mail that year.

2. **The Littlest Pet Shop Purge of 2016:** Upon entering my grown teenage woman years at thirteen, my first order of business was selling my large collection of plastic animal figures. I made it a mission to market them on my Instagram and had my mom help me make the most delicious, enticing eBay listings you've ever seen. By the time my whole collection was sold, I was three hundred dollars richer and had the business ego to rival a frat boy interning on Wall Street.

3. **High School Fashion Show:** Last but not least, I teamed up with a friend of mine to spend four months designing and sewing a seven-look fashion collection for our high school's annual talent show. It was the first fashion show our high school had ever had, and we cast our classmates as models, sourced the fabric from thrift stores, and practiced in my basement

before the big day. My after-school routine consisted of finishing homework and sewing until midnight almost every day. Winning "Best Dressed" my senior year never felt so right.

In high school, I liked staying busy. My role models were Elaine Welteroth, Yara Shahidi, and Shonda Rhimes; to me, they seemed to have it all together *and* had accomplished big things on top of that. So why couldn't I do the same? Plus, when people found out what a booked-and-busy teen I was, instead of seeing a developing workaholic problem, I got compliments like "You're so ahead for your age! How impressive, your future's so bright. What a determined young girl." And in many ways, they were right! All the time I put into my many activities helped me learn skills for success. However, after high school and the gap year I took, the transition to college gave me a jarring lesson on the difference between working responsibly for my future and pushing myself unhealthily.

When I started college, I already had two million followers on TikTok and a job as a host on TikTok Radio. My five-day college schedule competed with my radio host job, an exciting new commitment as a correspondent for Nickelodeon's *Nick News*, continuing to make TikToks on my own account, and attending branded events. Everything was go-go-go, and I rarely let myself sit down. After hosting for a brand during New York Fashion Week, I got an itch in my throat and ended up out sick with a virus for a week. My muscles started tightening up and my back was sore every night. I barely had time to call my mom, and it felt like I never drank enough water.

When someone would suggest that I take something off my plate, I'd express to them how grateful I was for the stress, because it was all from incredible opportunities that I'd dreamed about since I was a little girl. Saying no to a possible opportunity felt like sticking my nose up in the air Sharpay-style and acting like an entitled wannabe celebrity, so I said yes to everything I could. My jam-packed schedule lasted till the end of the semester, when I went home sleep-deprived, creatively drained, and still healing my warped sense of smell from when I got Covid during Thanksgiving. (Fresh bread smelling like pickles is wild. 0/10 wouldn't recommend.)

Wow, winter break must have been a lifesaver for you, Taylor! You finally gave yourself time to rest!

Reader, you won't believe what I did next. A week after Christmas, I hopped on a plane and visited friends for New Year's. I partied, went swimming in jeans (terrible idea), and caught the worst flu I've ever had in my life. By the time I got back home and my mom picked me up from the airport, I couldn't take a deep breath without hacking, which led to damaged vocal cords that wouldn't completely heal for three months. When we pulled into our driveway, I silently cried in the car and faintly whispered to my mom, "I can't move." I physically didn't have the energy to move my body and walk inside my own house. My mom half carried me inside. At that moment, a very frightening realization came to me: I had the ability to grind myself down so much that I could lose my autonomy.

The next week I stayed in bed doing absolutely . . . *nothing*. It was TERRIBLE. Sure, the looming headache and the high fever that made it impossible to sleep at night were uncomfortable, but what really scrambled my brain was being *forced* to turn my mind off and pause my plans.

I felt weak, lazy, and untrusting of myself. If I couldn't be strong and push through every life interruption without complaint, was I even strong at all? What I didn't understand was that I'd treated *my own health* and self-care as a frivolous, unnecessary thing by putting everything else first. When I could move around again without my fever returning, I promised myself that I'd prioritize creating safe spaces where I could feel vulnerable and at rest. Everything else would come second.

To this day, I am a go-getter. I still like a filled schedule, but now I know making time to be slow doesn't take away from my ability to be strong, nor does it make me ungrateful for my blessings. It shows that in addition to fighting tooth and nail for my goals, I fight just as hard for my well-being. If *I'm* not good, nothing I *do* will be either. There's a quote by educator Joyce Sunada that I love. She says, "If you don't make time for your wellness, you will be forced to make time for your illness."

This time in my life gives me perspective on how intense Ida B. Wells's emotions must have been as she decided what to do after her friend passed. I think about how much pressure she carried to continue her work without a moment to breathe and about how that pressure only increased as her life went on. Her story reminds me that no matter who you are—what your goals are or what stage of life you're in—you deserve to sometimes put down the rigid label of "strong," take intentional time to invest in your rest, and treat yourself with love.

Returning home wasn't an option for Ida. Her business partners fled Memphis. She was left with one thought: if they'd already taken everything away from her, she might as well keep telling the truth.

A few weeks before her thirtieth birthday, Ida published her findings about lynching in the South in a Black-run newspaper called the *New York Age*. The paper printed ten thousand copies of the issue with Ida's front-page article in it, and the cold hard truth of racism was spread throughout the country. The article even reached Frederick Douglass, who became a close friend of Ida's until his passing.

Taylor, this is all well and good, but, like . . . was Ida okay? This is a lot for one person to handle!

I often think about this too, reader. Ida B. Wells liked going to concerts in her spare time. She probably fangirled over the latest addition to her favorite book series. In the introduction to Ida B. Wells's autobiography, her daughter, Alfreda Duster, shared that even though Ida ended up married with a large family, people called her mother hard-hearted and unable to love, "but this was a facade: underneath she longed for the true love of a man she could respect and admire." Looking past her brave excursions and journalism, Ida was still a young woman who deserved to enjoy her life without the weight of a country's ignorance on her shoulders.

When I wonder what prevented her from breaking down and whether she ever took time to process all the pain she endured, I think of a moment she wrote about in her autobiography. While she was still in New York, Ida was invited to speak at a meeting hosted by some of New York's most prominent Black women activists, with esteemed Black women from New York, Boston, and Philadelphia attending. Doctors, writers, teachers, and more filled the room as Ida stepped to the podium. She shuffled her papers and cleared her throat. She looked out into the audience, who sat in anticipation. She breathed in and then breathed out the words she'd written on the page. She read aloud the same details she'd read over and over before, about the horrible things she saw in Memphis and the terrible losses she experienced.

But wait—this time was different. This time, her voice started to crack and her eyes started to well. A pang of hurt clamped her heart and tears streamed down her face. Midspeech, Ida's emotions poured out, but she didn't miss a beat in reading her testimony.

She showed up to that meeting not as an invincible warrior but as a real human being with complex emotions. In her autobiography, Ida describes this vulnerable moment as "weakness," but I see it as continuing her work telling the raw truth and fighting for its right to be heard. She deserved to honestly express her sorrow just as much as her anger. Everyone does.

Ida B. Wells dedicated the rest of her life to journalism. She became a potent spokesperson for Black women in the women's suffrage movement and aided in founding the NAACP. Yup. *The* NAACP. Ida B. Wells was *that* girl. She gave a new definition to "Strong Black Woman," and her story reminds me of something every strong Black woman should know: that alongside all the persistence, fighting, and work, she deserves to be soft, too.

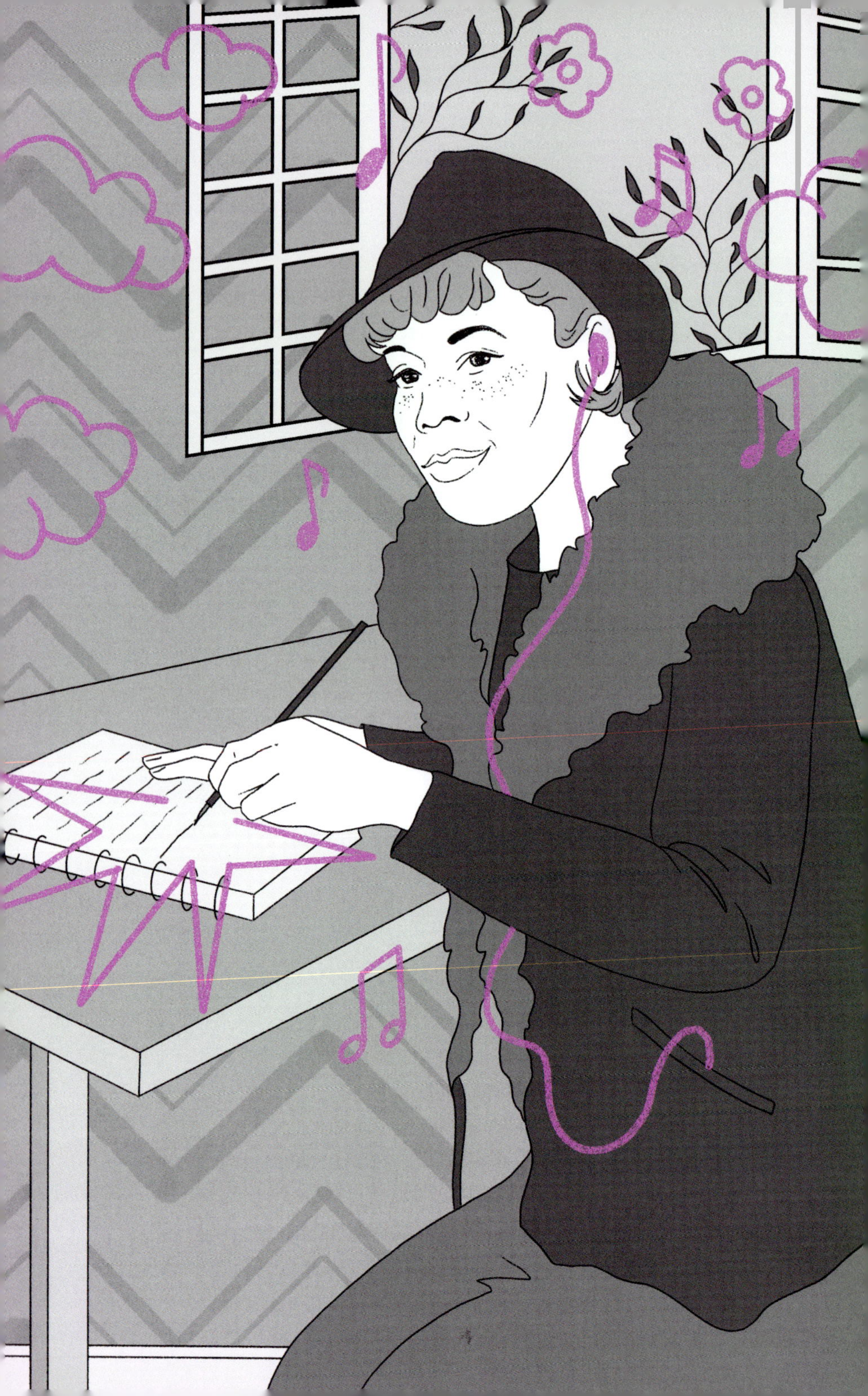

ZORA NEALE HURSTON
AND HOW TO EMBRACE YOUR COMPLEX IDENTITY

LET'S SEE IF YOU CAN GUESS THE PERSONALITY
of our next figure from a music playlist I made for her. See below:

Zora'z Songz
"**Her**"—Megan Thee Stallion
"**Just Fine**"—Mary J. Blige
"**So Fresh, So Clean**"—OutKast
"**I Will Survive**"—Gloria Gaynor
"**On My Mama**"—Victoria Monét
"**Flowers**"—Miley Cyrus
"**Independent Women, Pt. 1**"—Destiny's Child

"U.N.I.T.Y."—Queen Latifah
(who I think should play Zora in a biopic)
"Redbone"—Childish Gambino

Zora was that girl. End of chapter. Matter fact, end of book. Bye y'all. Stay safe. Unban books! Get money! Peace out!

Just kidding. Zora Neale Hurston was an author and is historically described as having controversial and bold viewpoints in her writing. In other words, her stories were *scandalous*! Once she started publishing books, her friends supported her art, but many of her fellow authors never saw the value of her work during her lifetime.

Zora was born in Alabama but moved to Eatonville, Florida, as a child. Eatonville would have major influence on Zora's writing because of its place in the South—and because it was one of the first towns incorporated by Black people in the United States. In fact, Zora's dad was the mayor of the town at one point! Black royalty for real.

Zora grew up surrounded by Southern culture, dialect, and folklore, which fueled her creativity and imagination. Zora graduated from a high school called Morgan Academy, got her associate's degree at Howard University, and then got a bachelor's degree in anthropology at Columbia University's Barnard College. And while Zora was stacking up degrees like a boss lady, she was also developing her writing style. She started studying at Barnard in 1925, which meant she was in New York at the height of the Harlem Renaissance.

To explain the Harlem Renaissance, let me tell you about Vine. When I was in sixth grade, I was introduced to Vine videos for the first time. Vine was a social media app where you could post skits, tutorials, and more. What was so cool about Vine? The videos were *only six seconds long*! This was my first introduction to short-form videos, and I was amazed! I had never seen anyone make jokes in such a small amount of time. I loved seeing the creativity people put into inventing new styles of video content for this new form of social media. People were able to bring their creativity to the public more easily than ever and on a larger scale than ever. I call it the Vine Renaissance!

In the 1920s, a similar thing happened in the Black community in the Harlem neighborhood of New York City. Only a few generations out of slavery, more and more Black people decided to leave the notoriously bigoted southern states in what became known as the Great Migration. They sought refuge in cities with more open-minded thinking. And many people ended up in Harlem. There was something in the air there—a new feeling of freedom, which brought new opportunities for art and creative expression.

Like never before, Black people started sharing art focused on their experience, much of it created in Harlem, and Black artists made money off their work. A new era of Black art emerged, defined by how honestly it depicted Black life instead of how well it pleased White audiences, as had been the case in the past. The phrase "New Negro" was used to describe the rising generation of Black youth who purposed their work for social justice and breaking stereotypes. When I hear "New Negro," I always think of Childish Gambino shouting, "Stay woke!" in "Redbone," and that's why that song is number nine on Zora'z music playlist. New creative mediums like jazz music exploded in popularity, and musicians like Louis Armstrong became successful across the country. Authors, musicians, and artists alike saturated pop culture with more Black expression and stories than the United States had ever seen before.

During Zora's studies, she made friends with young writers—including some who went on to become famous symbols of the Harlem Renaissance, like Langston Hughes, Countee Cullen, and Richard Bruce Nugent—and collaborated with several of them to create a literary magazine called *Fire!!* The magazine's purpose was to set fire to old ways of thinking about how African Americans should live and what they could be. The stories and articles were so controversial that the magazine was immediately in debt due to poor sales—and on top of that, the headquarters burned down, ending *Fire!!* after just one issue. (It's taking every melanin cell in me to not say, "*Ironic.*" So I won't say it. I'll publish it in a book instead!)

Zora really started to develop her voice as a writer when she traveled back to the South to do anthropology research, collecting African American folktales. She never published the collection of folktales she'd been planning, but she did start publishing novels inspired by her research. Zora's stories were about Black people, but they weren't centered around racism or fighting for social justice. She wrote about Black people's dreams and their desires to live a full life. Her words untangled the often-tortured depiction of the African American soul that had shown up in American literature before then, and put sweet salve into it.

I personally fell in love with Zora Neale Hurston's work in high school after reading one of her most popular books, *Their Eyes Were Watching God*. As the romantic, dreamy teenager I was, I thought her poetic words made life sound like a painting. At the end of the year when the teacher asked what book the class loved reading most, I was the only one raising my hand for Zora. I swear my head whipped around the room like, "Y'all still not hip to my girl yet!?"

With all my heart, I wish I could say that every person during the Harlem Renaissance welcomed Zora's words into their arms warmly—but instead, her writing was denounced, and Zora paid a high price.

TAYSTORY!

Sing it with me now. If you know it, you a real one:

**LIFT EVERY VOICE AND SINGGGG
TILL EARTH AND HEAVEN RINGGGG
RING WITH THE HARMONIES OF
BOX BRAIDING**

Taylor, don't you mean "harmonies of liberty"?

That was the old version. Ever since I finally mastered the art of doing my own box braids, the Black National Anthem has never sounded the same.

My parents raised me to take pride in my Black identity and to know things like the Black National Anthem (okay, the original version), and I was *fierce* in showing my love for my Blackness during high school. Anytime there was an essay assignment, I'd find a way to weave Black culture into it. For two years, I held leadership roles in my school's MLK Jr. Club, which met every week to talk about important aspects of Black culture, and I personally handed out club flyers to other students during the day. I participated in a high school competition with the NAACP called ACT-SO, where pride in who I am was drilled into me even more. One year, I even won our county's Racial Harmony Award for K–12 students. The message I was sending the world was clear and apparent: I'm proud of being Black! And don't you *dare* try to make me feel otherwise!

Buuuuttt pretty soon my intensity about Black pride became more of a hard-shelled armor than a confidence booster.

Because I was often one of only a few Black kids in my classes, if not the *only* one, I had to always be prepared for an uncomfortable question from a classmate or for everyone's heads turning to look at me when any type of civil rights discussion was happening. As a kid, being called names and having stereotypes pressured onto you means that you end up learning comebacks and defense mechanisms just to get through the day. For example, when a student called my hair dirty after finding out I didn't wash it every day, I'd respond, "At least my hair isn't limp and stringy." After summer vacation, when people held up their tanned arms to compare them to mine and said, "We're almost the same color!" I'd answer, "You wish!" I fought back by celebrating my Black identity before anyone else could twist it into something foul. That impulse protected me for a long time—but on the other hand, constantly waiting in anticipation for whatever rude thing a non-Black person might say to me caused me to make assumptions about people without really knowing them. It took one incredible teacher my junior year to break that guard down.

Remember that history class with the students' ignorant comments that pushed me to create *Fast Black History?* Can you believe it was also one of my favorite classes of the day? That's because it was the only classroom I could walk into where I knew the teacher would catch and address all the eyebrow-raising things I heard. He'd take the time to let every student share their opinion and then act as a moderator for students who wanted to respond—and boy, did I respond. He taught us how to have critical conversations about history in the context of our lives today and how to listen to each other with patience and open-mindedness. Plus, he was the only teacher who took my requests to include more diversity in the curriculum seriously. I felt seen—and safe enough to speak up in class to defend all the pride in my culture I'd amassed over the years.

But one day, as he joked with the class before the bell rang, he cheerfully brought up prom and said, in reference to our lesson that day and the fact that he knew I loved to design clothes, "We can all go in 1800s dresses! And Taylor can make them!" All eyes turned to me and I *clammed up.* All my Blackity Black senses started tingling, and I thought, *Is this a trap? I already know what kids will say. They'll say I wouldn't wear a dress or go to prom at all in the 1800s.*

They'll say I'd probably wear rags. They'll bring up slavery. So I responded a little too curtly: "I'm *not* doing that." I'm not gonna lie, I brought the mood down. My teacher looked at me knowingly, and I felt like he could read my mind. As I walked toward the door, he called me to stay back and gently suggested to me that although the truth of Black people during the 1800s exists, shutting out the entire era from my imagination was a little extreme. My face grew hot and I suddenly felt so embarrassed. That day I went home and wrote this in my diary:

> For so long my identity has been my race and culture. So, in a class full of White kids talking about slavery and learning from White historians, where is the balance between defender and open-minded? Moreover, what's it feel like and how will I obtain peace of heart even when White kids are debating culture and race like a science project?

Think of what it meant to be a "New Negro" in Zora's time period. For many, it meant shutting out everything from the past and moving forward into the future by fighting against racism. But when I donned my own version of this, I developed such a strict definition of what being "Black" should be that I clipped my *own* imagination of what Black people could do and experience. (For example, wouldn't it be exciting to read a story about a Black prom queen in the 1800s? This time I *would* want to design the dress!)

HAPPY PROM, CLASS OF 1800!

This moment in class completely changed the way I thought about Blackness. Instead of something to be defended, it became a world of opportunity. Rather than focusing so heavily on defensive comebacks and lectures to non-Black people, I started to ask more questions about Blackness and all the ways it could look. I firmly believe this moment is what pushed me to create some of my coolest *Fast Black History* videos, like the one about the Black Victorian princess Sarah Forbes Bonnetta, or the one about Bass Reeves, a Black deputy marshal in the American West. I learned that challenging your own beliefs when you learn a better way takes courage but can be the key to your best life. I see Zora as exuding this kind of courage; she explored *every* facet of what Blackness meant to her, and she accepted it even when it stepped outside the bounds of "New Negro."

When Zora was doing her anthropological research in the South, she studied real families and communities, learned about their folklore, and connected the dots to her own experiences as a child. The stories she amassed represented her life and the lives of many Black people who didn't have their honest perspectives written about in literature. When she wrote her own novels, her characters spoke the same dialect as the people she interviewed during her studies, which ended up rubbing many "New Negro" authors the wrong way.

The most successful authors of the Harlem Renaissance were praised for shedding light on racism and the struggles of Black people. Authors like Richard Wright of *Native Son* and George S. Schuyler of *Black No More* defied stereotypes from White-made media (which depicted Black people as bird-brained and slow-thinking) by creating analytical characters who criticized White supremacy directly. When Zora published a novel about Black characters without formal education, with a plot that focused on the main characters' relationships with each other instead of the fight against racism, let's just say it didn't immediately get praise for matching that "New Negro" energy.

Many people loved Zora's book, but others *loathed it*. There were even prominent authors who publicly spoke ill about her writing. Critics accused her of holding back history and feeding into the same old negative stereotypes about Black people's intelligence and way of speaking. When Zora's characters spoke, they did use broken words, grammatically incorrect sentences, and Southern slang—but unlike the White-made media that used this style of speech to convey stupidity, Zora used a character's dialect as a geographical marker of where they came from, as a piece of their life story. Saying she was feeding into stereotypes is like accusing someone who talks with a natural country accent of mocking someone with a country accent whenever they speak. It doesn't add up.

Zora's work would eventually go out of print, leaving her in poverty. She was buried without a marked tombstone. Her work was forgotten until the 1970s, when Alice Walker, author of the renowned book *The Color Purple*, read a book of Zora's that she borrowed from a neighbor. She fell in love with its poetic language and dialogue that felt like home. What was the book, you ask? *Their Eyes Were Watching God.*

After research, digging, and a trip to Fort Pierce, Florida, Alice Walker found Zora's grave and bought a tombstone for it with the words "A Genius of the South." Because of Zora's unflinchingly authentic picture of the South and the people who lived there, along with Alice Walker's passion for her work, Zora Neale Hurston is now known as one of the most important writers in the history of American literature.

What inspires me most about Zora is her openness to all kinds of perspectives on Black identity, as well as her faith in her own values. Even though prestigious authors (some of whom I imagine she might have been a fan of) tore her art apart, she stood by her work. She had the courage to create art that felt authentic to her *and* that captured her identity as a Black woman from the South in every bit of its complexity. Her work wasn't always popular, but it brought a sense of home to her and millions of others—and that was worth protecting against all the people who didn't understand.

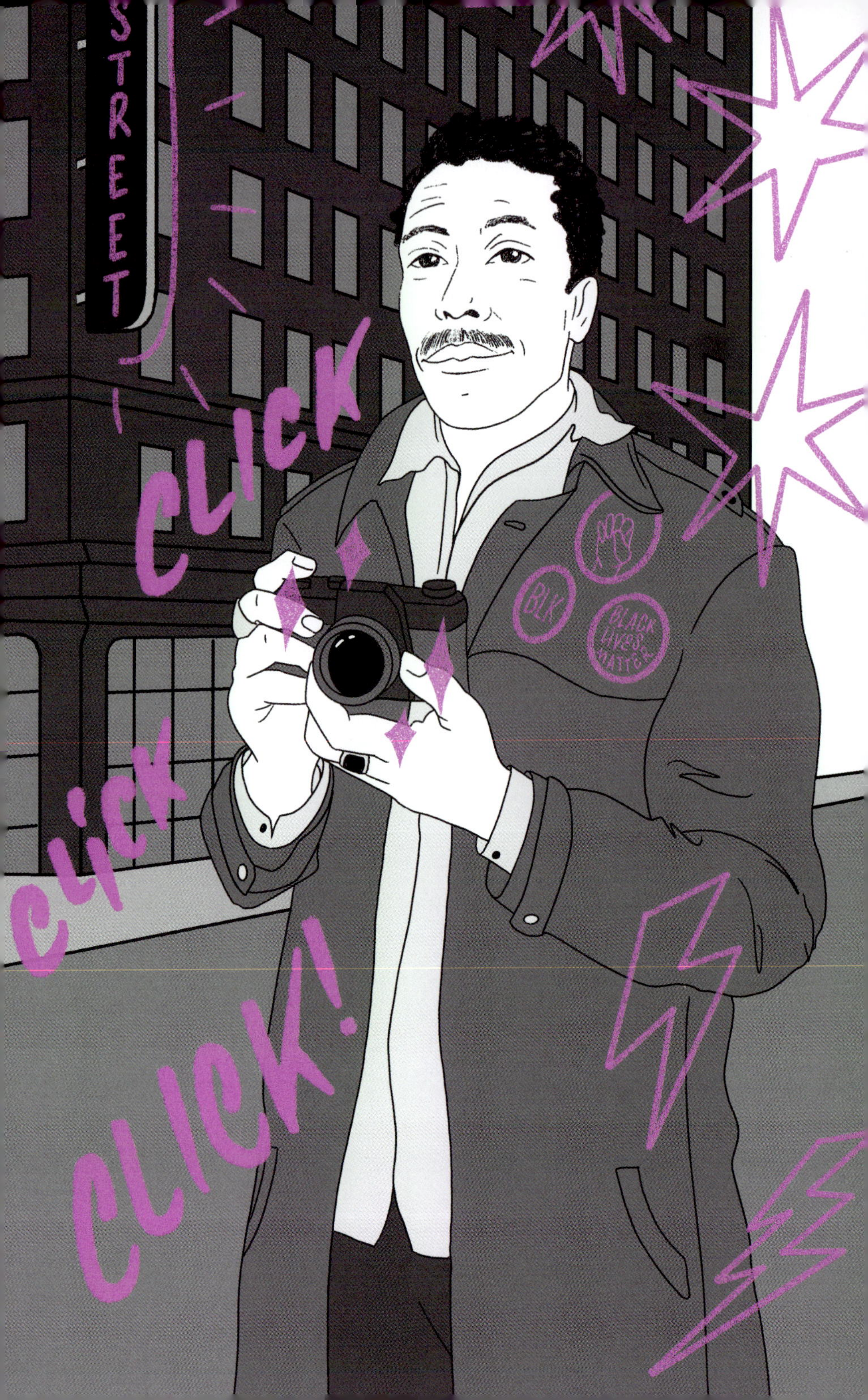
STREET
CLICK
click
CLICK!
BLK
BLACK LIVES MATTER

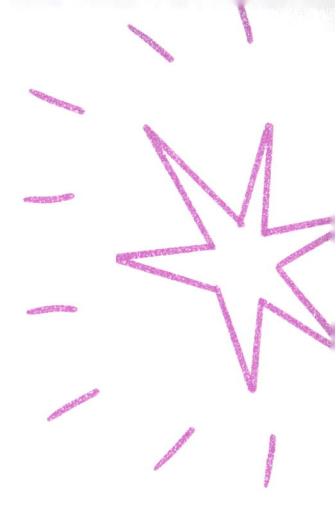

GORDON PARKS
AND WHEN IT'S TIME TO TAKE A RISK

ONCE UPON A TIME THERE WAS A MAIDEN WHO lived in a forest with her two evil stepsisters and her stepmother. She was forced to clean their mess and tend to them all like a servant. They treated her terribly and saw her as nothing more than a living dustpan. One day, all the village was invited to go to the royal ball—and with a magical fairy godmother's help, the poor girl attended in a bright blue dress that stunned the masses and attracted the prince. Having been nicknamed "Shoe-lock Holmes" the previous year after solving a theft by matching the suspect's shoe with a footprint in the mud, the prince found the poor girl after the ball using the glass slipper she left behind.

The girl married the prince and lived happily ever after. The girl's name was . . . well, you probably know her name. BRANDY!

Wait, you mean you *haven't* seen the ABC television special of Rodgers and Hammerstein's *Cinderella* with iconic music artist Brandy starring as the first Black actress to play the main role on-screen? Reader, we gotta get you cultured.

Now, I've always had some questions for Brandy (aka Cinderella). What happens after "Happily Ever After"? Does Cinderella wipe her hands and forget about all the other people stuck with evil stepsisters or even more wicked circumstances? What does she do with the power she has as queen of the kingdom, someone who could help those without fairy godmothers to speak for them?

While I never got to ask Cinderella these questions, I think I know how Gordon Parks would have answered them. He worked for success and a comfortable life, but he still chose to risk it all to be a reverberant, honest voice advocating for those who reminded him of his past.

Born in Kansas in 1912, Gordon grew up in a family of farmers. He and his fourteen siblings all worked on their parents' farm and attended school. But school wasn't exactly a safe space for Gordon. The area he lived in was so small that both White and Black children attended school together, but the students were still segregated. I can just imagine the tension between grade-school children being taught to look at other kids of a different race with either hate or fear.

Gordon's teachers consistently discouraged his hopes of

pursuing higher education and barred him from participating in sports and extracurriculars the way White children were allowed to. And even outside school, the horrors didn't end. When he was eleven years old, a couple of White boys threw Gordon into a river, believing he couldn't swim (and taunting him as they did). Even though the current fought with Gordon, he chose to stay hidden under the waves and let the boys believe he'd drowned, emerging safely on the other side when they'd gone. From early on, Gordon was taught that life was about survival and *making* your own way to a safe place.

When Gordon was fourteen, his mother passed away and he was sent to live in St. Paul, Minnesota, with one of his sisters and her husband. With grief freshly weighing on his heart, and surely missing his other siblings, Gordon had frequent arguments with his brother-in-law. Tension grew in the household. By the time Gordon was fifteen, they threw him out of the house, leaving him to fend for himself in the cold winters.

Now, y'all, winter in Minnesota is *no joke.* My family and I lived there when I was four, and although we didn't stay for a long time, I still remember the freezing temperatures—and my battle with pneumonia because of them. If I were Gordon, not even legally old enough to drive a car, without any money or shelter, I would have been scared out of my mind. Not only that, but the betrayal of family leaving him without support would have added to the already heavy grief Gordon was still processing. Gordon rode into a new chapter of his life confused, cold, and afraid of the unknown.

Ahem. He was *confused, cold, and afraid of the unknown! HELLO?*

Hmph, where's a fairy godmother when you need her, amiright?

Instead of waiting for a fairy godmother, Gordon spent his teenage years and most of his twenties being his own support system, hopping from job to job to make a living. He worked as a piano player, a waiter, and even a semipro basketball player. Seems fun, right? Not exactly. Having to continuously look for work as a teenager while *also* being his own parent must have been extremely lonely and difficult for Gordon. If I were in that situation, my biggest hope would be that one day I'd feel secure with a job and a life that brought me the safety I longed for.

Fast-forward to Gordon at twenty-eight years old, now with a wife and kids. One day, he saw a newsreel with photos of the sinking of the USS *Panay*, which was a gunboat that had been bombed by Japanese warplanes. In a 1964 interview with the Smithsonian, Gordon said, "I just plain thought it was exciting the way he captured these pictures and suddenly this new medium seemed like a possibility to me and I had been looking for all sorts of means whereby I might be able to express myself."

And *that's* when Whitney Houston, in her fairy godmother costume from the ABC television special of Rodgers and Hammerstein's *Cinderella*, shimmered in front of Gordon out of nowhere and handed him a camera, saying, "It's possible!" before she shimmered back out of sight. (No need to Google that, just trust me.)

Okay, no, he still didn't have a fairy godmother. However, the photos inspired Gordon so much, he bought his first camera for $7.50 and took a few photos of seagulls with his first roll of film. The more Gordon learned about photography, the deeper his passion grew. He'd photograph everything—his wife, people he met, his surroundings—to grow and develop his style. He knocked on stores' and businesses' doors offering his services, but he didn't find much luck—except at a boutique in St. Paul run by a man named Frank Murphy. At first Murphy's response to Gordon sounded like a familiar rejection. In Gordon's own recounting for the Smithsonian, Murphy said, "We get all our fashions done in New York . . . who told you you could shoot fashion anyway?" but Murphy's wife overheard the conversation and convinced her husband to give Gordon a chance. With that chance, Gordon photographed lots of models in the store's clothes and wowed the Murphys, who displayed his images all around St. Paul. And with that visibility, more work began coming in, Gordon started his own photography business, and soon he was a photographer for Marva Louis, the wife of heavyweight champion Joe Louis.

That's right, Gordon was on the up. If his childhood self were to look at him in this moment, he'd be amazed. So that was it! That was Gordon's happily ever after. He finally made it to a job he loved, and he lived comfortably with his wife and kids, without any more obstacles, forever . . .

. . . is what I would have said if this book was written to prank you. With a camera, Gordon held in his hands both the key to his success and a potential tool for positive change. The question was deciding how much of his newfound life he was willing to risk.

TAYSTORY!

Senioritis can take the fun out of many things. Especially if your senior year takes place completely over Zoom because of a global pandemic, like mine did. For the entirety of my last high school year, I was waking up every day at seven a.m. to stare at a laptop until three p.m. That could have been fun if watching a screen for eight hours meant binge-watching *A Different World* for the fifth time, but in my case it was mostly tedious days with teachers scrambling to mix up their lesson plans in a bid to keep students' attention. I've always tried not to fall asleep in class, but *you* try staying awake during an early-morning precalculus lecture while you're still cuddled up in your pj's in bed!

From my first day of school, my only thought was "Let's just get through this." I'd had an incredible junior year: I took some of my favorite and most difficult classes, ended up with straight As, went viral on TikTok, and started making money from my videos. As far as I was concerned, I had paid my dues to high school and I was ready to move on! But in the first couple days of senior year, one class challenged me in an unexpected way.

I remember being excited to start this semester-long course and *super* excited to meet the teacher, whom I'd heard so much about. Let's call him Mr. Man. For the last three years, I'd heard other students at my high school raving about Mr. Man—how "woke" he was and how laid-back his classes felt. I'd heard about how much he pushed his students to think deeper and really got into the nitty-gritty of his curriculum. Although she never actually took his class, my sister even interviewed him for a paper on race relations she was writing for a different course. That was all I needed to hear to register for his class.

As I sat down in the classroom on the first day (the classroom being a Zoom call in my bedroom), I eagerly awaited my teacher's arrival . . . and he arrived late. On top of that, within the first thirty minutes I was raising my eyebrow at his sudden, out-of-context, and critical opinions on wearing masks in public and having more open conversations about race, the way people had been doing that year. By the third day of class, he cemented my dislike with this generalizing comment: "People don't talk to each other about race; they yell at each other and flip each other off."

I'm the last one to police people's blunt opinions, but my

issue was that he didn't bring up his all-encompassing views to teach *better* ways of having conversations or to introduce any other sort of lesson. It felt to me like his comments were just for shock value, and I never really learned anything from them. Listening to him made me wonder if he'd watched even a single video out of the thousands made by people (including me!) who were working hard to open up dialogue about social issues in an accessible way. The semester continued and his comments increased, getting more alarming by the day. (Hey, by any chance are you short and stout? If I give you a lil push, will I pour you out? No? That's okay, but it's a good thing this story is, 'cause I got some tea to *spill*.)

During almost every class, he'd go on long tangents bragging about his "diverse" friends, telling us their real names, their gender identities, where they worked, and where they lived, occasionally sharing his screen to show us their Facebook pages. Who needs privacy, right? He'd frequently say hypocritical things about women and people of color, like when he said using the word "Whites" to describe Caucasian people was insensitive, even though throughout the semester he'd casually and frequently use "Blacks" to refer to Black people. When I'd speak in class, trying my best to ask questions that would clarify his thoughts in relation to the lesson, I'd receive off-topic rants about current politics. What upset me the most were the comments he made about students at our school from "lower" academic classes, or those who had disabilities, saying we should be "grateful" for our own lives in comparison to theirs. Finally, when I asked him politely in an email to incorporate his opinions more fluidly with the lessons and curriculum rather than just spew them at us, the next day he talked at length about how protesters in alignment with the Black Lives Matter movement were just "inarticulate" with the comment "I'll probably get an email about that." Words cannot describe to you how frustrated trying to learn in this class made me.

The more I tried to understand Mr. Man's teaching style and learn what was promised in the syllabus, the more it seemed his goal wasn't to challenge the way his students approached social issues or to connect bold statements with the history behind them. It was to air out his own feelings about society and his personal life. I wrapped up my first semester with some new friends who'd experienced the same frustrations with Mr. Man and with a burning disappointment that I'd learned next to nothing in the class.

The upsides were that I already had a decent grade to finish the class and that, while my school had gone back to in-person learning by then, it was optional, so I didn't have to come into school every day to see Mr. Man face-to-face. If I really didn't want to listen to him, I had the option to put him on mute from home (and I often did)! The past three years, I'd poured all my time and energy into academic competitions, clubs that promoted Black community, and even challenging the lack of diversity in my teachers' curriculums. As far as I was concerned, my due diligence was done. A deep and valid desire to give in to senioritis grew within me. I just wanted to coast through my last few classes quietly until I could be rid of Mr. Man's class forever.

But my fantasy of doing nothing started to crack when I'd think about the next semester and the new batch of hopeful students who'd feel just as disappointed as I did. I thought about all my work over the past three years, and I was reminded of the reason behind it. My goal had never been to "just get through it"; it was always to create positive change for those around me and those who would come after.

So I reached out to friends who'd previously taken Mr. Man's class. I asked them to tell me about their experiences and what they wished had been different. What I received were stories, photos, email screenshots, and voice recordings not only from *my* friends, but from *their* friends, all chronicling Mr. Man's behavior. It simultaneously excited and shocked me to see the number of voices speaking out, all of which had gone unheard by this teacher. Not only would he single out students from marginalized communities, he'd dismiss any complaints they had about feeling uncomfortable in his class.

I created an anonymous email and compiled everything in a thorough message to my school's principal. Here's a very shortened excerpt:

> I'm writing to you to address concerns from multiple students who have in the past or are currently enrolled in Mr. Man's classes. It is important to bring attention to the influence of his teaching style and unwillingness to accept well-backed criticism from students. Below you will find examples with explanations from others (identities anonymous). . . . It is distracting to learn in Mr. Man's classroom as these experiences happen. It causes students to not look forward to class. . . . These are not onetime instances. They have happened in the classroom often enough for it to be common knowledge among students. . . . The purpose of this email is for the above conduct to stop, as it affects student learning as mentioned. Thank you for your action and time.

DROP THE MIC! BOOM!

I have to be honest, when I sent that email I felt extremely nervous. Even though I kept everything anonymous, I had a fear that Mr. Man would still somehow find out it was me, one of his most outspoken students. And speaking up also came with the possibility of nothing being done to fix the problem. But even with these anxieties, it felt good to take the risk. It was brave to step out of a place of familiarity and safety to voice a wrong.

After a few short email exchanges with the principal, the best answer I got was "These have been received." Then there was radio silence. I never found out whether the school took real action toward Mr. Man by the time I graduated, but I was still glad to have amplified the voices of the students Mr. Man had ignored, even if doing so didn't get the desired result.

When you have a choice between trying to make change or staying comfortable, choosing the latter can sometimes mean choosing silence. And nobody can silence me. The lesson I take with me from that class, even today, is that life becomes more meaningful when you take risks for the things you care about. And as you'll learn from the rest of Gordon Parks's story, when you speak up for change, you can have a huge influence.

Gordon moved his family to Chicago, where both his business and his reputation as a skilled photographer grew. In addition to his fashion photos, he'd point his lens at the city, snapping shots of people of color in poor living conditions, which he then showed at exhibitions. His perspective placed a spotlight on those who were often written out of the narrative of American society in the 1940s.

Gordon's photos were so strong that, in 1942, he won the Julius Rosenwald Fellowship, a prestigious grant for Black creatives. This was a *big deal*, because Gordon was being offered funds and support for his photography with no requirements attached. He could *pick* where he wanted to work next—and the Rosenwald Fund would help him get whatever job he wanted. What a switch-up! Instead of going from job to job based on whatever he could find, now Gordon could have his preference.

If he'd wanted, he could have found an easy, well-paid gig that would allow him to save up money and secure his family's future. He could have lived the rest of his days taking pretty, easy-to-look-at photos that fit the brief and got him a paycheck. Who would have blamed him if he chose the safe, comfortable option? But that wasn't Gordon.

The photos that won him the fellowship were impactful not only because they said something deeper about poverty in Chicago, but also because they told the story of Gordon's own childhood. When he looked at the kids he'd snap pictures of, he'd be brought back to his life in segregated Kansas. When he saw the economic disparities around him, he'd be reminded of his struggles raising himself at fifteen. Gordon's heart was pulled to work for something more than a risk-free life. He wanted to make change. So he chose to work for the Farm Security Administration.

Who were they? Did they want him to photograph barnyards with American flags on them or something?

Wouldn't that be fun, but nope! Put simply, the FSA was created with the goal of helping farmers improve their poor living conditions. One initiative was a program that sent photographers to document America's poverty with the intention of using the photos in educational publications.

Gordon picked up his life and moved to Washington, DC, ready to take this next step in his career. However, he had to understand what he was up against. Before he took any photos, the FSA sent him to explore Washington, DC, and scope out the culture there. So Gordon went out to see a movie . . . and he was denied entry. Okay . . . that was new. He knew DC could get pretty cold, so he walked into the department store to buy a coat. They wouldn't sell him one. (In my mind, he left the store yelling to the employees, "Big mistake!") When he tried taking his son for a bite to eat, he was told, "We don't serve Negroes." Well, dang, tell me how you *really* feel.

Gordon came back to work furious about his experience, and rightfully so! After spending so many years in St. Paul and Chicago, which weren't as segregated as other cities, Washington, DC, was a culture shock. But that shock started a fire in him. He wanted to find a way to fight the bigotry he'd seen, and his weapon of choice was a camera. As he said in an interview with art historian Martin H. Bush, "What the camera had to do was expose the evils of racism, the evils of poverty, the discrimination and the bigotry, by showing the people who suffered most under it."

With his lens back in hand, Gordon spent the next several decades taking piercing photos that uncovered the truth of Black life in America. One of his first and most famous photos with the FSA shows a Black woman who worked as a maid at the

FSA's headquarters, standing in front of an American flag with a mop and broom and staring into the camera with a melancholy expression. When Gordon's boss saw the photo, he said something along the lines of "Wow, this is powerful, but you'll get us all fired!" This photo wasn't just a woman standing in front of a flag. It showed how the American ideal for Black people had them restricted to a life of service forever. That bold statement would *not* have appealed to many Americans.

Even with the risk of hate, Gordon got the photo published anyway, and it defined the rest of his career as someone who never sugarcoated the truth. Gordon continued to bravely document Black life with the FSA until the program ended. Then he went on to become the first Black staff photographer at *Life* magazine, where he published some of the most impactful photos of segregation and the civil rights movement available today. Never afraid of taking risks, he helped usher in the iconic film era of Blaxploitation by directing the hit movie *Shaft*, which put a Black character in an action hero role. For his lifelong work spotlighting the stories of Black people, Gordon was awarded the National Medal of Arts in 1988.

My favorite thing about Gordon is the way he saw the world as an ongoing story, one that we can mold and change through our decisions and beliefs. When the opportunity arose for him to be a light for others—and an amplifier of their voices—he never turned down the challenge for the sake of comfort. I try to take the same approach to life as Gordon Parks, answering every call for change in my heart with passion, ferocity, and intention.

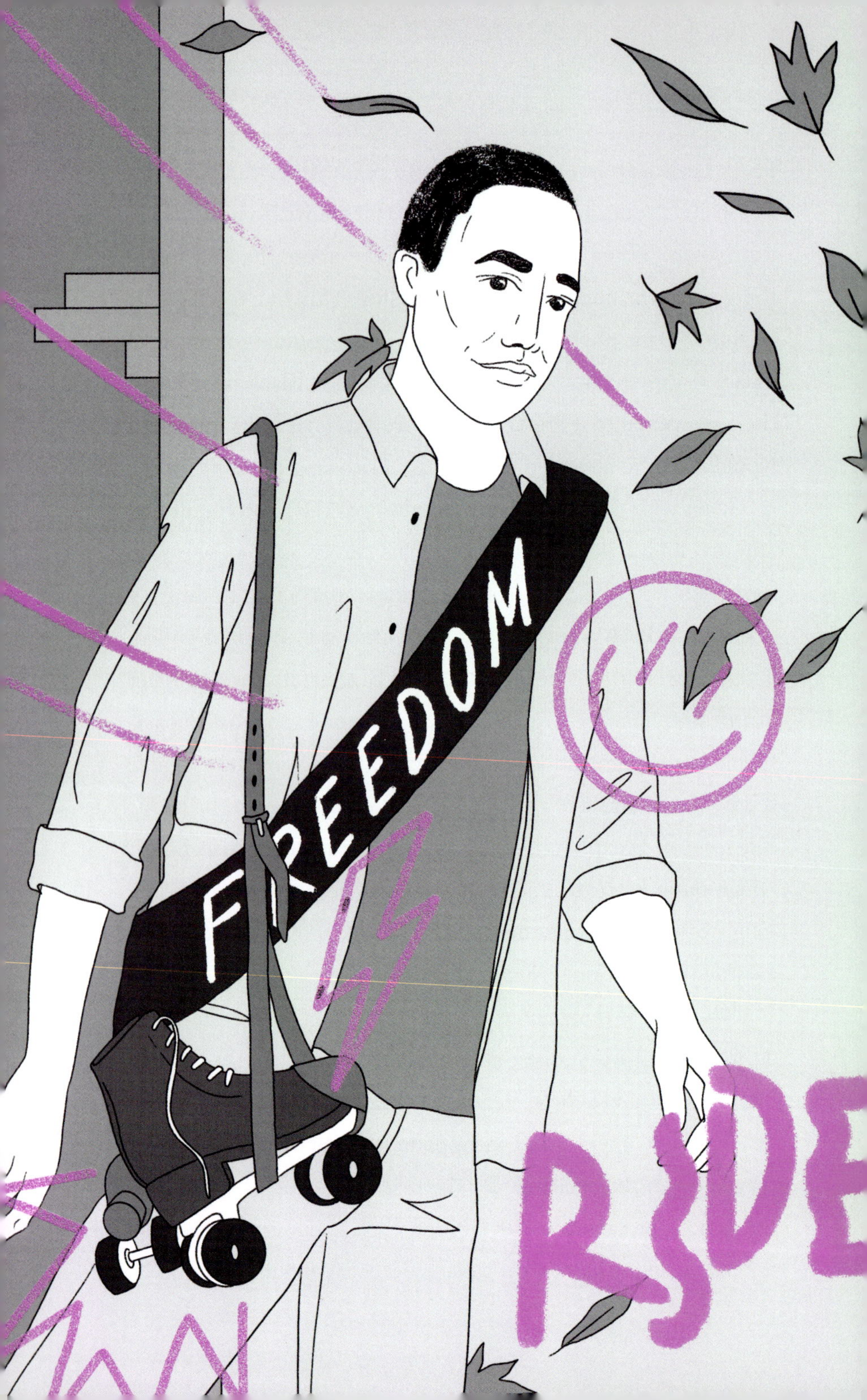
FREEDOM
RIDE

LEDGER SMITH
AND HOW TO FIND CONFIDENCE IN NERVE-RACKING MOMENTS

WHEN I WAS YOUNGER, THE SUMMER CAMP I WENT to used to take us to the roller skating rink every week. All of us kids would pile into a big ole van and crowd around the AC vents trying to escape the hot summer humidity. But once we walked into the building, the cramped ride over was so worth it. One of my favorite parts was when they'd turn on all the party lights, spin the disco ball, and play "Party Rock Anthem" by LMFAO. Everybody would immediately stop what they were doing, put down their half-spilled ICEEs and sticky arcade tokens, and rush to the roller skate floor. You should have seen it, man. There was an unspoken unity in a bunch of ten-year-olds who didn't know each other skating together to a very 2011 song, and it gave me so much joy. Even if I no longer drink as many ICEEs or eat as many lollipops from old vending machines, I will always think of roller skating as something that brings people together. And this chapter is about how Ledger Smith took that same idea and made a huge statement with it.

Ledger Smith was a semiprofessional roller skater who worked as an entertainer for celebrations and parties, often going by the name "Roller Man." (What would your roller skater persona be named? I'd probably go by "Wheel Nas X," "Scoot Dogg," or "Rollanna.") It was 1963, and Ledger planned to attend the March on Washington for Jobs and Freedom.

He wanted to attend the huh?

The March on Washington was organized by a man named A. Phillip Randolph. My guy had worked for civil rights and job equality for decades. He had even tried organizing a march about twenty years prior, in the 1940s, but he called it off after Franklin Delano Roosevelt (the president at the time) said he'd form a government committee and put out an executive order to protect Black people from discrimination at work. In the early sixties, when Randolph saw that the government was still failing to protect Black people's rights as promised and that the civil rights movement was gaining immense momentum, he and fellow civil rights leader Bayard Rustin teamed up with Martin Luther King Jr. to organize another march that would *not* get called off. This time, the goal was to pressure Congress into passing the Civil Rights Act of 1964, which would outlaw discrimination based on race.

Great! Now you're an expert on the March on Washington! Let's get back to Ledger.

One thing about entertainers is that we love a little drama. *A little pizazz,* if you will. And Ledger Smith was no different.

Ledger knew that the march could be life-changing not only for him but for his children and grandchildren, too. He knew that the world would be watching as the marchers challenged old systems of racism and discrimination and demanded a better society. With all this in mind, Ledger wanted to do more to participate in the march and stress to everyone just how important and historic this event was. The question was, how would he do that?

Ledger looked at what he had: two pairs of roller skates, determination, and a super-catchy stage name, Roller Man! And he made up his mind. He would roller-skate from Chicago to Washington, DC, to attend the march.

Great! Wait . . . What?

I know, right? I don't know about you, but when I run, it doesn't take me more than five minutes to run out of breath. I can't even comprehend what level of endurance I'd need in order to *roller-skate* across multiple states—I always gave my skates a rest after the first chorus of "Party Rock Anthem" played!—but that's how devoted Ledger was.

To train for the start of his journey, he ran five miles every day. He also contacted the NAACP and arranged to have cars follow behind him for protection. Finally, his departure day arrived: August 17, 1963. Ledger waved goodbye to his wife, whom he'd meet up with again at the march, and set out. From state to state, Roller Man skated, focused on his mission. Displaying the word "FREEDOM" on a sash across his chest, he waved to people cheering him on and wishing him luck. One could say he was on a *roll*. (Bad joke? Man, I thought I was wheely good at this.)

Imagine that you're at a restaurant, having a good grilled cheese sandwich, and as you gaze out the window you see a determined-looking man roller-skating by, with multiple cars following him. What would you think? If it were me, I'd be super curious about why he was on skates rather than in a car, what his sash symbolized, and why so many people were cheering him on.

That was exactly Ledger's goal: to grab attention and dramatize the march in order to get people thinking about why it was necessary. At the very least, the nation would see how far people were willing to go to fight for equality.

Although Ledger's journey was full of support, there were certainly struggles along the way too. Afterward, he recounted to the *Baltimore Afro-American* newspaper how, once he passed into Indiana, someone tried to scare him by almost running him over with their car: "There were a few nasty remarks. At Ft. Wayne, Ind., I almost got hit by a car. The driver drove up behind me. Then he stopped the car all at once." At that moment, Ledger would've had a good reason to give up, step into one of the cars following him, and ride the rest of the way to DC. After what he had already endured, no one would have blamed him! Instead, he *chose* to stand by his message, even in the face of fear. That's what put that pizazz in his journey.

TAYSTORY!

I think it's time to tell you about how I managed to channel the same type of confidence as Ledger—and maybe how you can find that confidence too.

From Ledger's story, we've seen that, when you have a big goal or believe strongly in a particular message, there will always be someone who disagrees with you. Sometimes those people might try anything to silence you, and you'll have to stand alone. Ledger understood all this going into his roller skating marathon. He decided that his willingness to do good was more important than his fear of not being accepted. In other words, if Ledger were here today, he'd say, "Don't trust the haters, homeslice." (. . . Maybe not in those exact words.)

But for me, and maybe for you, learning that truth raises a new question: What if the haters *aren't* other people? What if the voice discouraging and silencing you . . . is your own?

Let me paint a picture for you. It's the first day of school. The outfit you spent the night before choosing is laid out on the bed. As you change and get ready to start the new year, you're full of confidence. You think to yourself, *I look so good. I changed my hair from last year, I got a new shirt, and my backpack has five pockets. Five! Everyone's gonna want to be my friend!* But when you walk into class for the first time, faced with all new people, all that confidence feels like it suddenly abandoned you for a vacation at the beach.

That's how I felt when I was invited to my first TikTok content creator event. The excitement on the plane ride from St. Louis to Los Angeles was unreal, and checking into our hotel room felt like a dream. I was on top of the world. But when all the other TikTokers started showing up to the event space and it was time for me to join them, suddenly a pit formed in my stomach. I literally left the hotel elevator, walked to a corner in the event space where no one in the crowded room could see me, and ran away back up to my hotel room after two minutes!

I'd been invited by TikTok to attend, and I knew that was because the videos I made were great, but I still couldn't help but feel like I wasn't good enough to be there. In those two minutes at the event, I'd seen so many creators I loved, some of whom I even grew up watching. Seeing the contrast between my few months online and their years of experience made me believe for a moment that I was just a high-school girl from the Midwest who had crashed someone else's party.

When I told my mom, who had come on the trip with me, she said to me, "You will go back downstairs, talk to other people, and be yourself. You don't need anything else but yourself." And that reminded me of how I got to this amazing event in the first place.

The way I made my content and shared my passion for Black history wasn't successful because I pretended to be someone else or copied another person's ideas. My videos were impactful because when people watched them, they saw *me*—my quirks, my excitement, and my humor. I realized that to make a good impression and have a great time at this event, I didn't need to be funnier or more outgoing or have more years of experience. All I needed was to show up and continue being what I'd always been: me!

I hugged my mom and went back to the event space,

this time with a better mindset: if they don't like me, that's okay. Either way, I'll know that I stood firm in who I am.

When I stepped off the elevator it was like God saw that my heart was ready. Immediately I met a creator I already followed, and we geeked out over each other's videos. That turned into another creator, then another, and soon I was making videos and bonding with half the creators at the event. Much to my relief, we were all treating each other like a community, and after facing my self-doubt, I felt at home being myself. The event ended up being instrumental to how I moved forward as a content creator. Imagine if I had stayed in my hotel room the entire time! I felt so proud of myself for choosing to confidently take a risk.

When I think about Ledger Smith, I imagine all the doubts he probably had at the beginning of his journey: "Roller skating? That's crazy! No one's going to pay attention to that! How goofy would I look doing something that silly?" But he proceeded despite those doubts. Just like I found the bravery to go back into the content creator event by shifting my mindset, Ledger also learned how important it is to water the inner thoughts that help you grow. Yes, there might still be haters, and your own discouraging thoughts might not go away completely, but remember that you are able to *choose* what messages you give power to in your mind—so that no one, not even yourself, can keep you from beautiful life-changing experiences.

That's amazing, Taylor, but we want to know: Did you meet any celebrities?!

Why, reader, I am so glad you asked. I'll have you know that I accidentally walked into Tyra Banks's photo session. She smiled at me with kindness, I did that awkward little duck you do after blocking someone's picture, and then I went into the bathroom and flipped out. So yeah, we're basically best friends now.

On August 27, 1963, ten days after Ledger began his journey, he and his well-worn roller skates arrived at the March on Washington at last. I can picture Ledger seeing the Lincoln Memorial and practically flying toward his finish line, his wife opening her arms to welcome him as he skates closer to the crowd.

Ledger attended the march and experienced Martin Luther King Jr.'s iconic "I Have a Dream" speech, Mahalia Jackson's performance of "How I Got Over," and the urgency of John

Lewis's call for freedom, along with 250,000 other marchers who were just as dedicated to stressing the importance of civil rights.

What makes me super pumped about this story is that at first glance, all Ledger did was roller-skate. But in doing so, what he *really* did was take his unique talent and passion and use it to make an impression on people, driving them to support his message. Even when it was scary to stand alone (and exhausting to skate for hours every day!), he was confident in his skills and knew he could measure up to the challenge.

That's what I want you to take away from Ledger's enormous feat. The skills you already use on a daily basis have the power to change someone's life positively. There's no need to try to make yourself look like someone else, or to fit yourself into a box. Heck, you don't even have to roller-skate (unless you *wheely* like ICEEs). To create history—and support your family, friends, and community like Ledger did— all you need to start is *you*.

I HAVE A DREAM! I HAVE
HOW I GOT OVER HOW I G
I HAVE A DREAM! I HAV
HOW I GOT OVER HOW I
I HAVE A DREAM!

DREAM! I HAVE A DREAM! I GOT OVER HOW I GOT OVER HOW I HAVE A DREAM! I HAVE A DREAM!

RECORD-BREAKING RUNNING MAN!

TOMMIE SMITH
AND HOW TO KNOW WHO'S ON YOUR TEAM

IT WAS A DARK AND SPOOKY HALLOWEEN NIGHT. China Anne McClain's "Calling All the Monsters" was in the top ten charts of nine-year-olds everywhere and my soldier costume was bedazzled and ready to be shown to the entire neighborhood. I had my mind on candy and candy on my mind. With each house my sister and I trick-or-treated, the sun sank lower and the air became crisper. The warm-colored autumn leaves were whisked away by the cold wind.

We decided on a big house with ghost decorations. I was talking about my hope for a king-size Kit Kat to my sister when one of the ghost figures suddenly moved toward me. Lebron

James's ankles would have twisted the way I pivoted on my feet. I was a runner. I was a track star. But my mom caught me midstride, and the ghost took off his head, becoming a regular suburban man. He handed out candy to my sister with an amused smile on his face. I decided that was the start and end of my track-and-field career.

Thankfully, an embarrassing prank on Halloween night wouldn't have stopped Tommie Smith from running. He was a professional track-and-field athlete with the kind of determination that not only brought him record-breaking speed but also drove him to make a powerful gesture at the 1968 Olympics—one that had harsh consequences for him but still commanded the world's attention.

If you've played a sport, have you ever been named MVP (Most Valuable Player)? Usually, this is the person who saves the team in the last moments of the game or always encourages team spirit. Tommie was the MVP *and* the GOAT (Greatest of All Time). During his time in high school, he played basketball, football, *and* ran track. In track, he set so many school records that some of them still haven't been broken decades later. On top of this, our man was voted vice president of his senior class! If I made a movie about his life, I'd put in a scene where he's striding down the hallway wearing a letterman jacket and holding a track-and-field trophy, and then the principal busts out of a locker, cartwheels toward him, and crowns him king of the school while confetti rains down from the air vents. Just when the bell is about to ring for the first period,

Tommie puts his hand on the shoulder of the school bully and says, "Come on, Billy Bobinson. You can't get a jump start on life by running away from your problems." And then everyone claps. I don't know about y'all, but I'd watch that movie!

Tommie's speed didn't stop with high school. When he attended San José State for college, he ran the 200 meter straight in 19.5 seconds. That's running the length of *four Olympic swimming pools* in less time than it takes me to sing half of Nicki Minaj's verse in "Monster." Setting a college-level track-and-field record that wouldn't be touched for another *forty-four years* was more than enough to put him on the right track (pun very much intended) to travel to Japan in 1967, where he participated in an international competition for college athletes called the Summer Universiade.

What cheer would you scream for Tommie if you were a friend supporting him at a track meet? What do you think would hype him up? I know if it were me, I'd bring ou*t bars* and I don't mean gymnastics. Here's the poster I would have held up in the stands for Tommie:

★ TOMMIE, TOMMIE, YES HE CAN, ★ THE SPEED OF LIGHT CAN'T CATCH OUR MAN!

So, what medal do you think Tommie won at the Summer Universiade? *Gold.* And Tommie Smith did not intend to slow down, so are we really surprised he made it to the Olympics the next year?

Now, this Olympics didn't happen during an ordinary time. Let me set the scene for the year 1968:

You're walking to your favorite candy shop like you always do after school, and a group of people in front of city hall make your ears perk up. They're holding signs protesting the war in Vietnam, chanting with such vigor that you can't help but feel the unrest. Continuing your mission, you arrive at the store and find the Smarties hiding in between the Bub's Daddy bubble gum and the Tootsie Rolls. Before heading to the register, you peek through the shelves, eavesdropping on a conversation between the clerk and a customer. You can't see their heads, but the customer is waving their hands around in distress.

"Peace is a rare thing these days. And just when you think things are settling down, another tragedy comes at you," says the customer.

"I understand you. This year is *rough*, you hear me?" the clerk responds.

He hands the customer their Jolly Ranchers while the customer rambles, "I mean, first we lost President Kennedy, and now Dr. King? When will the violence stop?"

The clerk shakes his head, agreeing. "It's devastating. At this point, I just want to hear some good news."

As the clerk turns up the radio and Marvin Gaye's "I Heard It Through the Grapevine" fills the store, you bring your candy to the counter and spot a magazine with the cast of *Star Trek* on it, not knowing that soon the show would make history by airing the first interracial kiss between a Black woman and a White man on American television. Long story short, political and social tensions were thicker than a well-made sweet potato pie (candy *and* pie in one paragraph? I think I'm hungry). On top of the Vietnam War and the assassinations of John F. Kennedy and Martin Luther King Jr., the civil rights movement still demanded the nation's attention as well.

Going into the 1968 Olympics, Tommie recognized that he had an opportunity to use his platform to call for change. For that he needed someone he could trust to stand with him no matter what.

TAYSTORY!

Who's your best friend? No, wait. I have a juicier question. Who's your *ex*-best friend?

I met mine in kindergarten when I pointed out our matching pink jelly shoes in church. From then on, she was my *best friend*, okay? We decorated Bible covers together, hung out at the youth retreats, slept over at each other's houses, and even created two homemade comic book series about mythical creatures in composition notebooks. They were totally original and completely unique from each other. The first was about two mermaids. One was a princess and decided to live life on land, while the other ran (or I guess swam) away from her evil stepmother. Their meeting revealed that they were long-lost sisters the whole time.

Wow, Taylor, that should be your fiction children's book debut!

I know, right? The second series was about two fairies. One was from a wealthy fairy family and decided to live outside the forest, while the other escaped from an evil stepfather and ran (. . . flew) away. When they met, it turned out they'd been long-lost sisters the entire time!

I know what you're thinking. But I promise they were vastly different: one was drawn in my friend's notebook and the other was in mine!

Life couldn't have gotten any sweeter—until it did, in fifth grade, when I found out that my best friend would be switching to *my school*! It was like I was living my Dork Diaries fantasy! We could make the school our domain: give our crushes code names, gossip about teachers, and spread our best-friend energy through all the hallways! I was so ready to have more time with her and be even closer than I thought we already were.

But once school started, the energy changed. She wanted to hang out with me less and stopped responding to my hotmails (yes, I refuse to call it Outlook). By the time the annual church youth retreat came around, I'd been gently told by another friend that she'd been making fun of me behind my back, calling me names and gossiping about the way I looked. *No, my friend wouldn't do that! She's my best friend!*

I talked with her about it and she denied it. She promised she'd never mistreat me. I believed her. But when the retreat started, it seemed like she was avoiding me. I didn't spend time with her the entire trip—except for the part where I was wrongly accused of talking back to a power-hungry church leader, who decided to yell in my face military-style, and she was there and didn't say a word. (Guess who's the one who *really* talked back?)

We barely spoke over the next few months—or rather, *she* didn't speak to me. Having given her the title of "best friend" for five years, I was ready to fight for our friendship. When I was ten years old, I didn't have much understanding of what "ghosting" meant or what an unhealthy attachment to someone was, so I'd email her every day with long updates about my life, even though there was rarely a reply. Here's a real email from me to her in 2013:

```
hey....since camp ive felt like ive
been ignored..... today at church I tried
to smile at you and you immedietly turned
```

> away. . . . and when I was talking to you on the phone, we were in the middle of a conversation(ithink) and you immedietly said bye. I mean I know you were watching Another Cinderella Story, but you could have told me that you were watching it , can I call you later. im not trying to be mean. another thing, when we go back to schoolwill you promise me that this will be the best grade weve had in elementary school. even if we are in the different class.......

Y'all . . . I felt like I needed to beg her to be friends with me. Reading this also shows how far back my love affair with using ellipses for dramatic effect goes.

Eventually, I moved out of state and stopped texting my ex-best friend after I realized she wouldn't fight for me. The ending of that friendship taught me that having mutual love for mythological beings, pink jelly shoes, and gossiping about crushes wasn't enough to build a relationship I could really trust. We lacked *teamwork*. When there was a problem, I was always left trying to fix it on my own. Our priorities and ideas about how a friend should be treated were vastly different, and that gap between us was what made our connection crumble.

Taylor, back up! Are you telling me you lost your best friend right when you moved to a completely new place?

Yes, and going to school knowing no one and having no close friend to vent to, even long-distance, was TOUGH (Taylor Operating Under Great Hindrance). However, letting go of my "best friend" turned out to be a blessing in disguise. It taught me how to find people worth trusting—including a spunky, kindhearted girl I met in seventh grade who showed me what fighting for friendship *actually* looks like. I still keep in contact with her to this day!

What Tommie Smith did at the Olympics shows me that he knew the same thing I learned from my ex-best friend: when you're looking for someone to be on your team, good communication and collaboration are way more important than just having interests in common.

New Character Alert! Enter John Carlos, another student from San José State, who made the Olympics in the same event as Tommie Smith. Not only did Tommie and John know each other, they were also both part of an organization created by a professor at their school called the Olympic Project for Human Rights, or the OPHR. The OPHR's goal was to confront the discrimination displayed at the Olympics and shed light on racism in all sports.

It had only been about thirty years since Adolf Hitler hosted the Olympic Games. And in the years since, the Olympics hadn't made much progress toward equality. In 1968, the president of the International Olympic Committee (IOC) was Avery Brundage, who was known for refusing to boycott the 1936 Games in Nazi Germany when he'd been president of the US Olympic Committee.

Before the 1968 Games, the OPHR proposed that all Black athletes boycott the Olympics unless their demands were met. They wanted more Black people added to the US Olympic Committee, more Black coaches at the Olympics, and Avery Brundage removed from the IOC. They wanted Muhammad Ali's boxing title restored. (It had been taken from him after he refused to fight in Vietnam.) And they wanted the IOC to uninvite South Africa and Rhodesia from the Olympics, because both countries' governments had racist policies known as "apartheid," which had caused thousands of deaths and enraged people of color everywhere.

The IOC did agree to withdraw their invitations to South Africa and Rhodesia, but the OPHR never gained support for their other demands, and the boycott failed. Tommie and John were on their way to the Olympics after all.

Tommie and John were competing in the same event and had both supported the boycott, so they must have trained and worked together often because of this. However, they were complete opposites. Tommie was known for being more reserved and careful with his words, while John had a fierce personality and shared his opinions boldly. They weren't close friends before the Olympics. In a piece about them in *Sports Illustrated*, Tommie's wife described them as "oil and water." But with the boycott not moving forward, Tommie and John had something in common. They both wanted to use the Olympics as a platform to support Black human rights. So they planned their own protest.

At the 200-meter final race, Olympians from all over the world got ready at the starting line as the audience cheered. Tommie stood next to his opponent, John, his mind laser-focused and his breath steady. This was it. This was their moment to show the world all their hard work and talent.

The race commenced and they were off. Our man Tommie started the race a little behind his opponents, but near the end, a burst of energy pushed him past everyone and across the finish line in *first place*. Tommie raised his arms in celebration, and the arena erupted for two reasons. They cheered because Tommie won, and because his winning time *broke an Olympic record*. Are we even surprised? This is *Tommie Smith* we're talking about! He was the picture of victory and on top of the world.

★ TOMMIE, TOMMIE, YES HE CAN, ★ RECORD-BREAKING RUNNING MAN!

But not every victory comes with applause. There was such a contrast between the stadium's fancy decorations and state-of-the-art equipment and the people of color back home who were being mistreated while no one batted an eye. Before walking out to receive their medals, Tommie and John agreed on a plan that would take advantage of the world's eyes being on them—and put them both in an extremely vulnerable position. This plan required no words, but Tommie did need a few other things.

WHAT TO BRING FOR A MAJOR HISTORICAL EVENT AT THE OLYMPICS

1. Gold and Bronze Track-and-Field Medals

There's no better way to protest racism and show the ability of your people at the same time than wearing a medal that screams "Victory!"

2. Black Socks, Ditch the Shoes

Systems like segregation and redlining (a practice where mortgage lenders refused to give loans to people in neighborhoods with mostly people of color) have prevented Black people from having equal opportunities to build wealth. To represent those in poverty who have the system to thank for their position, wear black socks with no shoes.

3. Beads around Your Neck

Remember the victims of lynchings with beads around your neck, and keep the world's eyes on these murders that have devastated the Black community.

4. Black Gloves

A raised fist in a black glove is a symbol of Black power and Black unity. To show solidarity with Black dignity, wear black gloves. If you and your partner only have one pair, wear one glove each.

5. OPHR Pin

Remind the world of who is behind you, and of everyone fighting for your cause.

6. An Ally or Two to Stand beside You

This will be a pivotal moment not only in your career but in your life. Don't do it alone. Stand with your teammate, John. And when your fellow medal winner from Australia asks for an OPHR pin to support the cause, give him one.

Tommie and John both worked so hard to qualify for the Olympics. Tommie had been running track nearly his whole life to arrive at this point. And he was about to risk his entire career with someone he wouldn't even ask for advice on which pair of new kicks would suit him best. He could have ditched his teammate at the last second and accepted all the glory that came with an Olympic win. He might have been praised and given sponsorships and fame. But Tommie knew what truly mattered.

John and Tommie may have had differences in personality and humor, but what mattered were their values. Both knew the seriousness of their protest and understood how much more impactful it would be to stand beside each other in support. Yes, they were like oil and water, but together each one strengthened the other's purpose.

As they took their places on the victory podium, Tommie and John lowered their heads and raised their fists. *The arena went silent.* In an interview with *Runner's World,* John recalled the silence being so deafening he could have heard a frog pee on cotton. Now *that's* quiet. No one could pretend they didn't see. No one could ignore the clear message. The statement had been made.

Obviously, Tommie Smith and John Carlos received standing ovations and were celebrated all over the world immediately! They became best friends forever, and racism disappeared like a well-done lace front and everyone yelled simultaneously, "Thanks, Tommie and John!"

EEERRR. No. That's wrong.

Tommie Smith and John Carlos were expelled from the Olympics and sent home. They were criticized by the media and received death threats. And to top things off, even though they found jobs as football players in the NFL for a time, and later as coaches at various schools, they never competed in the Olympics again. They weren't really close friends after the Olympics either, appearing at events together only rarely.

Taylor, this . . . this is sad. What's your point with this?

My point is that even though Tommie Smith and John Carlos lost their Olympic careers, it was their mutual partnership that kept their values and aspirations alive. They might not have become BFFs, but when they put their fists in the air together and bravely called attention to human rights, they showed the true meaning and importance of teamwork. If they hadn't supported each other in their desires to resist, their entire careers might have been built on the regret of doing nothing. I learn from their story that to judge someone based on conflicting personality traits robs me of the opportunity to find out whether our values truly align. And if they do, I can always trust that we'll show up for each other when it really matters.

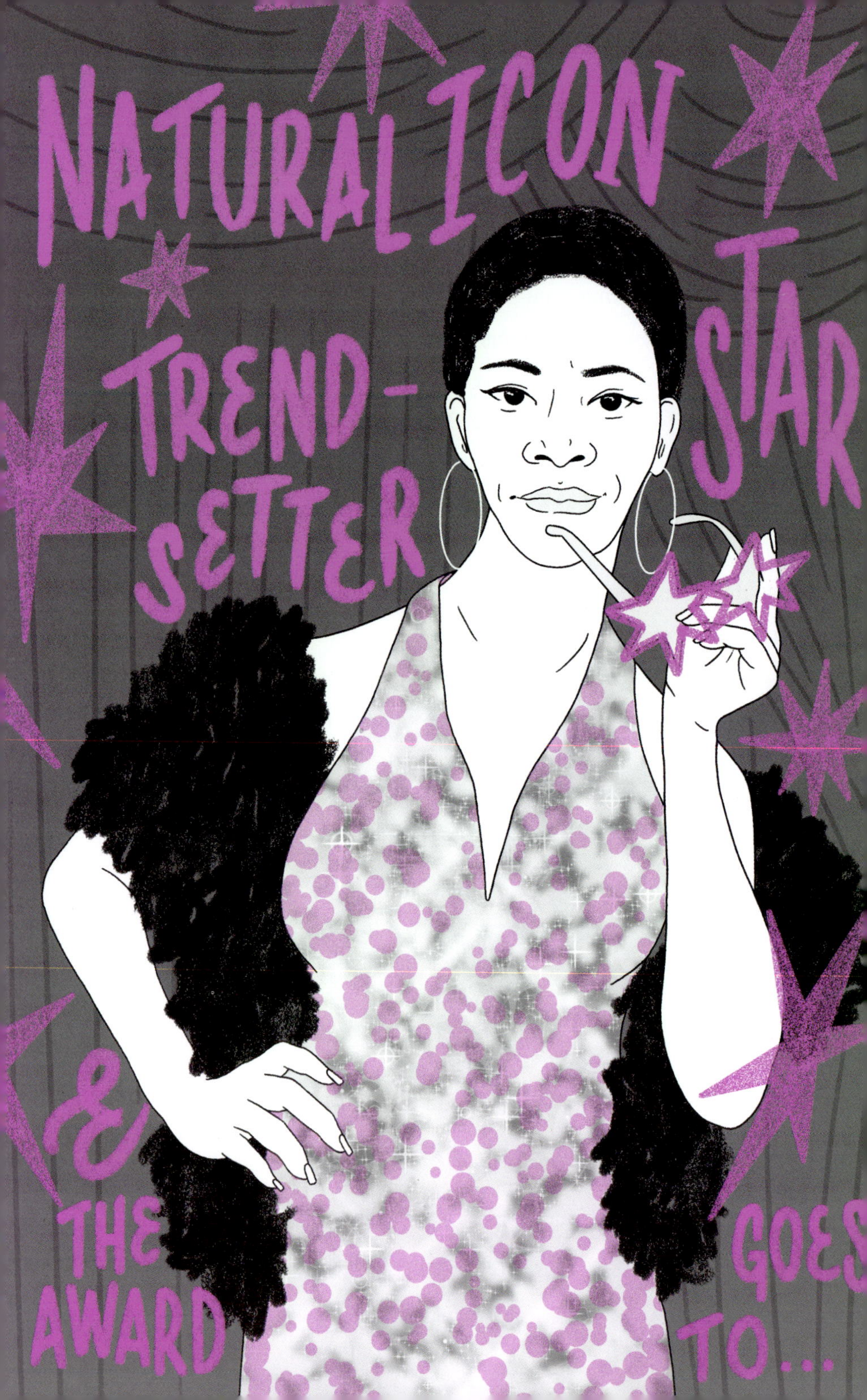
NATURAL ICON
STAR
TREND-
SETTER
&
THE
AWARD
GOES
TO...

CICELY TYSON
AND WHY GOOD REPRESENTATION CHANGES LIVES

WHO'S YOUR FAVORITE MOVIE CHARACTER? WHAT about them makes them your favorite? It doesn't have to be deep. You can like them simply because their outfits are cool or because they can swing from the tops of skyscrapers (Spider-Man, if you're reading this, *I love you*). Think about that character, and I bet that deep down a part of you loves them because in some way you either feel just like them or you want to be like them. Ooh, and I bet you've even tried once or twice to copy their fashion or dance moves, or you've memorized their catchphrase. Don't worry, I do the same thing! The shows and movies we watch affect our likes and dislikes, ways of seeing the world, and most importantly, ways of seeing ourselves.

I'll give you an example.

When I was in middle school, the live-action *Beauty and the Beast* movie came out and I went to see it with my friends. I thought it was pretty good! But one of my friends, who happened to resemble the main character, was *bawling* with emotion. There I was in the movie theater, waiting for her to pull herself together over watching a princess spin around in a floofy yellow dress. I remember thinking to myself, *I liked when the teacups and candlesticks sang 'Be Our Guest' as much as the next person, but it wasn't* that *good. If it was, I'd be crying too!* I was so confused as to how there could be this much fuss over one character. It was just a movie!

It wasn't until many years later, when I watched an animated short film called *Canvas*, that my opinion changed. *Canvas* was about an old man remembering his peak years with his late wife. By the end of it, I was in shambles. Here I was, crying the same way my friend had over a film less than ten minutes long. The difference? This film connected with my heart from the very beginning because the old man and his family were Black. Not just in skin color but in culture. I found myself pointing out things around the house he lived in, saying, "My grandparents had that too!" I looked at the detailed way the old man's hands were animated and saw my own granddad's hands. When I looked into the face of the granddaughter, it was like a mirror.

For the first time, I knew what it meant to find a deep, positive connection with a character I related to—and to truly feel seen in a movie. That, ladies and gentlepeople, is called:

✧ Representation. ✧

Nowadays, there are all kinds of characters and stories that reflect the diversity in our world. However, it wasn't always this way. In the United States in the 1800s, "minstrelsy" was a popular form of entertainment. This was when performers would cover their faces and bodies with black shoe polish, then sing, dance, and act like a stereotyped version of a Black person. People would perform songs like "Jump Jim Crow," which made Black people the butt of jokes about laziness, uncleanliness, and other negative traits. Most of the time, Black people were characterized as subhuman, or "not as human" as people who were White. Ain't that crazy? Even when minstrel shows started to fall out of trend in the early 1900s, humor that was based on making fun of people of color continued to be a standard in entertainment (yuck).

But, Taylor, I've seen Black people in old movies! Wasn't that representation too?

That's right! Black people were cast in movies starting in the early 1900s. However, even though having Black people on-screen in mainstream film was a huge advancement, they were usually only given subservient roles like the main character's maid, slave, or servant. That, or they were just extras in the background.

Now, don't get me wrong—there were many Black filmmakers, like a man named Oscar Micheaux and another named Noble Johnson, who made movies depicting Black people in more positive ways, but their movies weren't supported in the same mainstream way as majority-White productions.

Go back to your favorite movie character. How would you feel if someone said you reminded them of that person? I'd feel pretty good. But I wouldn't feel all that great if, instead, someone said I reminded them of a character from the movie that was looked down on or not even remembered. That's what it's like to be Black and only see images of people like you on-screen that are inaccurate and written by someone who doesn't understand your life experience.

Okay, Taylor. Great. Now I'm sad.

Then let's talk about how all of this began to change. How did we get from watching people making fools of themselves in blackface to screaming, "THAT'S MY BEST FRIEND!" in the movie theater as Lupita Nyong'o and Zendaya gracefully bless the Marvel Cinematic Universe with their presence? (Wait. Y'all didn't scream that?? Just me?)

One of the first actresses to break these barriers and challenge the played-out narratives of Black people on-screen was Cicely Tyson. Cicely was, with no exaggeration, a legendary actress. She knew what she wanted to achieve and wasn't afraid to put her all into making it happen.

On December 19, 1924, Cicely was born in New York to parents who came to the United States from Nevis, an island in the Caribbean. She was raised in Harlem during the Harlem Renaissance. Once she grew older, Cicely began working as a secretary—but the repetitiveness of this job made her super bored. In an interview with the *Washington Post*, she said she started thinking, "God didn't put me on the face of the earth to type for the rest of my life." It was the same routine *every day*. Where was the adventure? Inspired by how many people told her she looked like a model, Cicely decided to start modeling outside of work.

She began booking jobs immediately! Not only did her looks have flair, but so did her personality. Cicely soon quit her secretary job to go to modeling school and then became a top model in under a year. Our girl had magic, and magazines wanted her. If you walked into a store during that time, you might have seen Cicely in the spreads of *Ebony*, *Jet*, and *Our World*, all of which were major magazines made for Black women.

In an interview with *TheWrap*, Cicely shared the story of the next step in her career: She'd just finished a meeting with an editor at *Our World* magazine. Walking out of the office, she happened to catch the eye of an actress waiting in the lobby. I can imagine Cicely walking gracefully past and the actress feeling a gust of wind clear her mind and a light bulb go off above her head. *Ping!* The actress went straight to that editor and recommended Cicely for a part in a movie she'd auditioned for herself, saying that Cicely's look matched what the director wanted (*the* definition of women supporting women!!).

Sound the trumpets, throw the confetti, and perform your best TikTok dance, y'all, because Cicely's got her first movie!

HOLD ON.

When the editor told Cicely about the role over the phone, she hung up in refusal! Like I said, Cicely was the kind of person who knew exactly what she wanted. And she had no intention of acting in a movie.

WHAT? Taylor, I thought you said Cicely was an iconic actress!

I promise Cicely *did* become an iconic actress! But at this point, Cicely didn't love movies. As a child, she was *scared* of movies, after seeing *King Kong* and having nightmares that woke her up every night. We all had that movie as a kid that scared us to death (never show me Disney's *The Black Cauldron* after midnight). Think of yours. Now imagine if *that movie* was the very first one you saw in your life.

One word: traumatizing.

Also, keep in mind that the rise of movies and TV didn't rub everyone the right way. Many people, including Cicely's family, thought they were just a big parade of vanity. Imagine how wary Cicely might have been of her family's opinion of her—and the world's judgment!

Even with Cicely's opposition, the editor persisted. Eventually, Cicely agreed to meet with the director, who asked her to simply read the script for the movie. *Just read the script? No filming or acting or anything? Fine,* Cicely thought, *I can do that.*

The movie was called *The Spectrum*, and it was about a dark-skinned Black woman falling in love with a light-skinned Black man and having to face the struggles that came with that in the Black community. Once Cicely reluctantly picked up the script, she was riveted. She couldn't put it down. Whatever doubts she had in her mind were overcome by an inner fire from the storytelling.

Maybe there *was* something important about being in a movie.

She agreed to meet with the director again and read lines with another actor. In her memoir, Cicely described that first acting experience as "otherworldly, supernatural, and having inexplicable ease." You see, folks? This is it! This is the spark of a legend walking into their path.

The Spectrum was never released in theaters, but Cicely was hooked. She dove into movies and the off-Broadway scene, pouring herself into the characters and storylines. Productions like *The Blacks* and *Carib Gold* surrounded her with other icons, like James Earl Jones, Maya Angelou (who you'll hear more about in the next chapter!), and Ethel Waters.

Once she was cemented in the entertainment world, Cicely got a call from her agent to be in one episode of a TV drama on CBS called *Between Yesterday and Today*. Just like she did with every role, Cicely studied and dedicated herself fully to her character. This time her role was an African wife who wanted to hold on to her culture after arriving in the US. Now, Cicely wore her hair straightened, like many other Black women at that time. However, Cicely deeply cared about being authentic to the story she was telling. So one day, she walked into a salon and had the stylist cut all her hair off and revert it to its natural state. She believed this would accurately show the values of her character—even beyond her spoken lines.

After playing the role, Cicely was called back onto another CBS show, called *East Side/West Side*, to play a secretary. Cicely chose to keep her hair in its natural state for that show too. That decision is what got her into news headlines. By wearing her natural hair in a TWA (or a "Teeny Weeny Afro"), she became not only the first Black woman to have a recurring role in a television drama but also the first to wear her natural hair on television. Double whammy!

In her memoir, Cicely said that after that role, she got letters from hair salons about how all their clients wanted to copy her hairstyle. One letter said, "My clients want to have their hair cut off like the Black girl on your show!" For many people who looked like her, Cicely was the representation they needed to embrace a part of themselves that they'd never explored before.

READER! It's time for your favorite segment. Drumroll please:

TAYSTORY!

Like I've told you already, my sister and I mainly learned about Black history from our parents, and my favorite way that they taught us that history was through movies. Watching the actors on-screen portraying events that truly happened made it feel like I was taking a peek inside the memories of the actual people. Movies were what made Black history real and tangible for me. So when I was sixteen and heard about a short-film competition going on at my high school, I knew I had to compete. And I knew immediately the story I wanted to tell.

    I wanted to make a film about growing up and becoming more confident in myself as a young Black woman. You already know I was proud of being Black, but for years there had been bullies and haters at school who criticized the type of clothes I wore, how I talked, and what kind of music I listened to, simply because I didn't fit into their expectation of what a Black person is "supposed" to be. It seemed like I was "supposed" to know the name of every rapper, always wear hoodies, and under no circumstances "act White," which I apparently did by loving the show *Doctor Who* and saying in middle school that my favorite song was "Bohemian Rhapsody." Having these interests didn't at all mean that I was rejecting my Blackness, but when other kids looked at my skin color and saw that my personality didn't match the box they'd put Blackness into, they turned to bullying.

If you are being bullied for having unique interests, know that you aren't alone and you've done absolutely nothing wrong. On the other hand, if you're Black and your favorite music artist is Megan Thee Stallion, your dream is to be a basketball player, and you love wearing your lucky blue hoodie to school every day, that's still amazing! Those things just didn't fit with my personality at the time. (Let it be known, however, that Megan Thee Stallion is now a good 50 percent of my music library.)

It took years of work and relearning to understand that being Black didn't mean fitting into stereotypes and avoiding any interests that didn't fit into a box someone else made for me. The more I stopped letting shame keep me from being myself, the more I met other Black people who *also* had lots of different interests—and I learned that the best thing about being Black is that you can dream, like, and be anything you want!

Even though I was 100 percent sure this was the short film I wanted to create, it was still very scary to go through with it. Doubts ran through my head: *I don't know if I can do a good job. What if people don't understand? Will this even be relatable to anyone?* But in those moments, I encouraged myself by remembering people like Cicely Tyson, who gave so many audiences positive representation for the first time. By making a film about this part of my own life, I was creating positive representation for anyone who *could* relate—anyone who was also struggling with not fitting into a box, who needed to see that reflected on-screen in order to embrace all the things that made them unique.

Just like Cicely, I put my all into the project. I wrote the script, found the actors (aka my closest friends and my science teacher!), directed, and produced—all within the span of three months, so I didn't miss the submission deadline.

The late nights were all worth it once I could watch the entire short film to completion. I remember feeling like I let out the world's biggest breath of relief. I'd done everything in my power to create a film that wasn't just *finished* but that also had the potential to comfort someone experiencing the same struggles I'd gone through. I absolutely went into my room and did a little happy dance alone in front of my mirror.

However, what I didn't realize was that the hardest part of the short-film competition was just getting started. Sure, I had finished the movie, and I was extremely proud of it! But now I had to wait to see what others might think of it, and if they'd understand the message I'd worked so hard to share. On competition day, when all the contestants' films were shared in front of a huge crowd, I sat in my seat

> shaking so hard with nerves that you'd have thought it was below freezing in the room.
>
> As you continue reading, think about the scary feeling of sharing a part of yourself in a way no one's seen before—and how Cicely Tyson did that over and over throughout her career.

One of Cicely's most iconic roles was as Rebecca in *Sounder*. The movie was about a husband and wife, Nathan and Rebecca, who were struggling to provide for their family as sharecroppers. Cicely's performance led to her being nominated for Best Actress at the Oscars (pretty awesome!!) and sparked an impactful conversation about representation during the press tour for the movie.

Recall how I said there *were* many Black creatives in movies and entertainment but that our own depiction of ourselves was still rarely accepted outside the Black community. Many people only watched TV or movies written by White people, and as a result, they only saw Black people the way those White writers portrayed them. Once *Sounder* was released and Cicely went on the press tour, she saw the consequences of this in action.

As she talked with reporter after reporter, Cicely heard what people truly perceived Black people to be based on what they'd seen on-screen, and she saw their shock at how *Sounder* challenged those beliefs. In her memoir, Cicely quotes one reporter saying, "I didn't know that Black men and women had the kind of loving relationship that we see between Nathan and Rebecca. Their connection didn't seem believable to me." This reporter basically said she didn't believe Black people had the ability to truly love each other! Can you imagine how Cicely felt after working so hard on this film and waiting to hear what people thought of it—only to hear them say something like this?

Think about it: if all your life you didn't have relationships with, or even close proximity to, Black people *except* for what you saw on TV and in movies, you'd believe that whatever you saw represented was true. This reporter most likely grew up only seeing Black people represented in subservient or negative roles on-screen, so imagining two Black people in a loving and healthy relationship that she could empathize with seemed *absurd*.

Are you starting to understand why positive representation is important?

Cicely understood, and she deeply internalized this lesson. From that point on, she decided to dedicate her career to *only* being involved in projects that uplifted the perception of Black women on-screen. She went on to play many more iconic roles, including her Emmy-winning starring role in *The Autobiography of Miss Jane Pittman* and her Emmy-nominated performance in an episode of the historic television drama *Roots*.

Cicely's mission meant she had to reject several roles she was offered because they portrayed Black women inappropriately—as nonintellectual or lazy. But by making that sacrifice, Cicely changed what it meant to hold space as a Black woman in the entertainment industry. Her career success spanned decades.

She won three Emmys, a Tony in 2013 for Best Performance for a Leading Actress in a Play, a Peabody Award in 2020, an honorary Oscar in 2018, and in 2016, the *Presidential Medal of Freedom* (the United States' HIGHEST civilian honor!), presented by Barack Obama himself for her impact in entertainment.

Cicely Tyson used her time in the world to reshape how Black people are portrayed on-screen. Her resolve aided in changing the stereotyped narrative of what Black women could be, and she paved the way for her successors—actresses like Viola Davis, Angela Bassett, Zendaya (GO, BEST FRIEND!), and many more. And she did it with an endless sense of style! Cicely passed away in 2021, but her legacy will live on for countless generations.

TAYSTORY!

YO, TAYLOR. Did you win the short-film competition or not?!

Imagine if I never told you. Don't worry, though, I'm a good author! I won't leave you on a cliffhanger!

When my short film started to play in front of the crowd,

I tried to mask how nervous I was. As the first pivotal scene appeared, I heard a few gasps in the audience. Then, when the first joke in the dialogue came, the room burst into laughter. When my main character was feeling sad, I could hear whispers of empathy around me. And finally, when the film came to a close, I felt my entire body erupt with tingles along with the crowd's cheers.

I'd done it! They liked it! And they'd felt the same passion for my message that I had.

One of the most important memories I have from that day is of another girl approaching me after the screening. She talked to me excitedly about how much she related to my main character, how she'd gone through the same experiences, and how good the film made her feel. In that moment, all the fear and doubt left me, and I knew that I had the power, just like Cicely Tyson, to change people's lives by making them feel represented.

In the end, I didn't win that competition—but when I entered my second short film a year later, I won the silver medal.

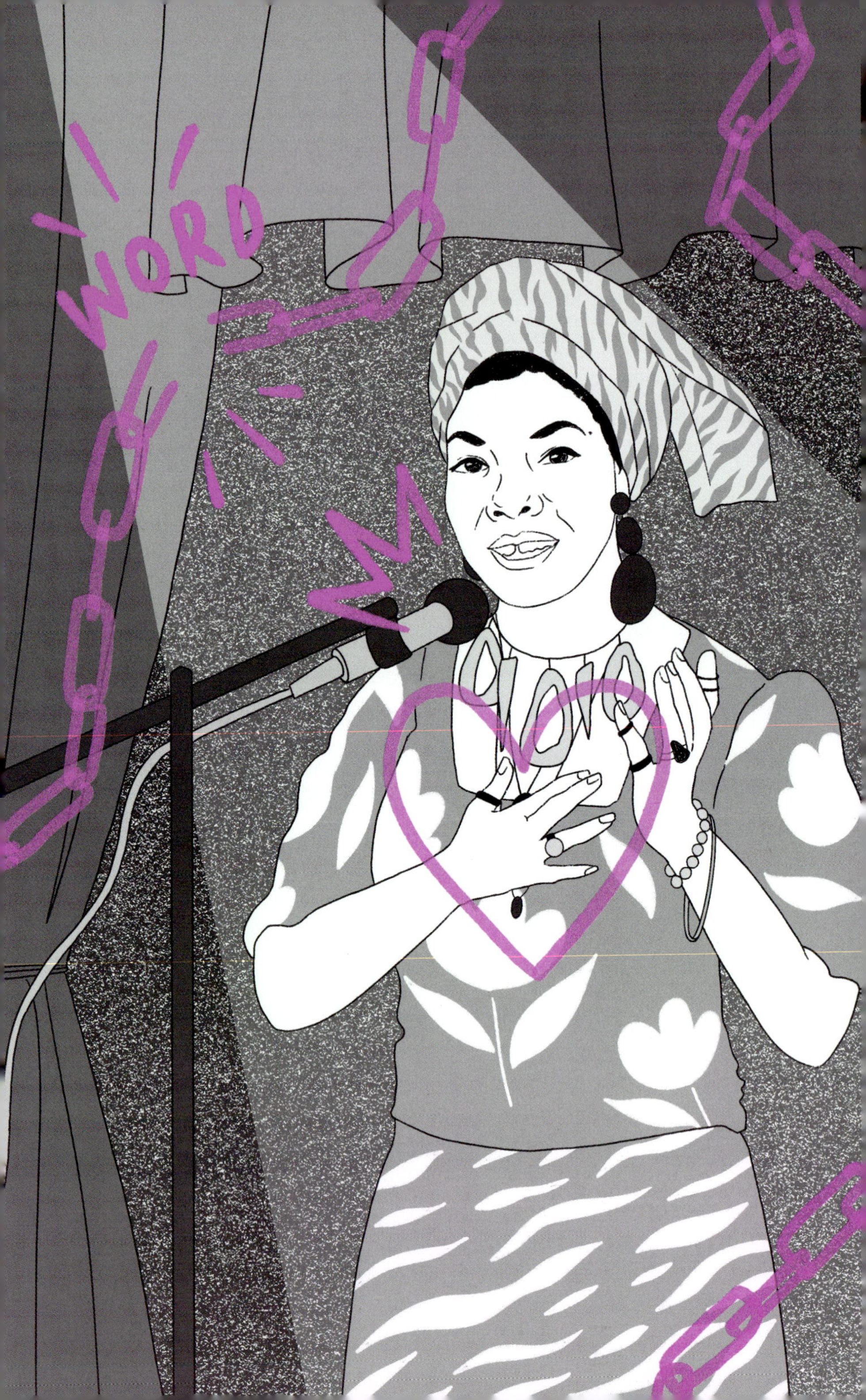
WORD

MAYA ANGELOU
AND WHY YOUR ENERGY IS NEVER TOO MUCH

WAIT!

This chapter includes discussion of Black trauma and violence. Read at your own risk—or if you need to, go ahead and skip this chapter. No hard feelings! We all must protect our joy sometimes.

"OH, MY LOVE. A THOUSAND KISSES FROM YOU *is never too muuuucccchhh.*" Ahhh, I love using chapter titles as an excuse to sing Luther Vandross. I also love reciting lyrics to said song in the voice of Maya Angelou to give it some *drama*.

If you've ever heard Maya Angelou speak, you'll know her voice *very* well. She's the author of famous books like *I Know Why the Caged Bird Sings* and poems such as "Still I Rise," and before she passed away in 2014, she did some readings of her work that were so good, she won *three Grammys* for spoken word. You can't help but listen to her recordings over and over when you find them.

Maya Angelou is my biggest role model, and one of the greatest adventurers I've ever learned about. The twists and turns of her life remind me of my grandmother, who loves to casually drop personal experiences that have immense historical significance. Like that one time during dinner when Nana nonchalantly said, "That's just like when I went to school with some of the Little Rock Nine," and then asked me to pass the mashed potatoes (and close my mouth before it started catching flies).

If Maya's life were a movie, here's how I'd write my online review:

RATING:
★★★★★

YOOOO!! SHOUT-OUT TO ST. LOUIS!! I know she was only born there and spent most of her childhood in Stamps, Arkansas, but I'm still excited she was born near where I'm from. Also?? Getting a job and making history at sixteen as the first Black woman to conduct a cable car in San Francisco just because you liked how the uniforms looked?? Icon. Energy. Only.

One of my favorite parts was when

she started singing, dancing, and gaining fame. Do you *know* how cool you have to be to *turn down* a Broadway lead role to tour internationally in Europe with another show instead? Sis knew her priorities for real. Also, have you ever gotten married, moved to Egypt, and become one of the only Black women journalists for a newspaper there? *Me neither, but Maya did.* And listen, the cinematography when she came back to the US to keep working for civil rights, then became close friends with Martin Luther King Jr., wrote seven autobiographies, and won three Grammys actually made me ascend to Heaven. During the scene where she became the first Black woman to have her screenplay adapted into a feature film, I think I should've left the theater because I was definitely screeching "BOW BOW THAT'S HOW IT'S DONE!" It's giving side quest warrior in the best way.

    My only problem was when they chose that slow, sentimental song for when she was awarded her Presidential Medal of Honor. I personally would have chosen "On My Mama" by Victoria Monét, but I guess art is subjective or whatever.

While it's not certain whether I'll ever see a musical biopic of Maya Angelou where the actress does the choreography to a Victoria Monét soundtrack, it *is* certain that Maya's life was an incredible journey full of extraordinary accomplishments. When Maya expressed herself through words, she opened the world's eyes to what it was like to have a pre–civil rights movement childhood and grow up to live a full life in spite of that. Her voice changed lives—including mine! But what would have happened if Maya never spoke at all?

Let's look back to Stamps, Arkansas, in the mid-thirties. Maya and her little brother live there with their grandmother, and they've just returned from a trip to see their mother in St. Louis. Except eight-year-old Maya comes back different from when she left: she doesn't speak anymore.

The cause of her silence lived in a trauma she experienced while in St. Louis, when a family friend took advantage of her in an evil way. After Maya told her family what the man had done, he was murdered. As a little girl with only a small understanding of the world, Maya connected the only two dots she had: her voice = death. She believed that when she spoke about the wrong done to her, she became the sole reason for the man's death. Maya didn't say a word for the next five years.

What a heavy conclusion for a little girl to make.

I agree, reader. Maya should never have felt the need to blame herself for another person's actions.

Have you ever had a teacher or authority figure ask you to point out the person who did something wrong? Even if that person broke a rule, maybe even if they intentionally hurt you in the process, there might still be a feeling of anxiety and guilt that comes with telling the truth. You might feel like your speaking up or not is the only difference between them receiving a punishment or walking free. So maybe, to cope with that burden, you refuse to say anything at all. For Maya, this fear must have been heightened in a way I can't even comprehend.

Over the next few years, her silence was a constant reminder of what she'd gone through, but it also heightened her love of books and poetry. Maya did very well in school and scored high grades—at least when her assignments didn't involve speaking. She read anything she could get her hands on and spent time memorizing texts. Give her Shakespeare? She was on it. Hand her Edgar Allan Poe or Charles Dickens, and she'd eat it up. It's almost like how, to this day, I can perform dances from the Nintendo Wii's Just Dance video game series from memory, except I memorized less Shakespeare and more Nicki Minaj!

But all those texts Maya memorized? She only recited them in her head. She still wouldn't dare speak. So Maya started to blend into the background of her own life and, as she described in her memoir *I Know Why the Caged Bird Sings*, "sopped around the house, the Store, the school and the church, like an old biscuit, dirty and inedible." For fear of causing disaster for others, Maya threw away the key that locked up her personality and freedom. It would take someone very important in her life to show her that living is most enjoyable when you set *all* of yourself free.

TAYSTORY!

Hey, shawty, wyd? Nothin'? Aight, das cool. Me either. Well, maybe I'll see you, maybe I won't. If you hit me up, I might be busy, idk.

Oh, you're busy later? Idc. Whatever.

That was me doing my best impression of a nonchalant romantic interest. How'd I do?!

If being "cool as a cucumber" means both having too much green in your closet and being nonchalant about life, I've only got one of those down. If you've seen any of my videos online, you may have noticed the vast number in which I'm bouncing off the walls with energy, yelling loving affirmations, or (my personal favorite) dancing to R&B music while dressed as a Black historical figure. My energy is chaotic, and that intensity pours into my whole life—especially my friendships. Let's recap with a list:

TAYLOR'S TOP 5 EXTRA MOMENTS IN FRIENDSHIP

1. Getting a buddy's friends and family to film personal videos for me to compile, edit, and send to her the morning of her birthday.

2. Making my mom drive around to every Pier 1 Imports location in the area to find a very specific penguin statue my friend saw on a commercial once and mentioned she liked.

3. Sending an entire cardboard cutout of Harry Styles to a couple of friends in a different state for Christmas.

4. Writing a custom funk song for my sister and singing it to her on her twenty-third birthday.

5. Sewing a dress that looked like Angelica's from *Hamilton* from scratch for my theater-loving pal in middle school.

(Honorable mention: sewing my friend's cat a skirt for its birthday.)

Once I start to trust a new friend or connection, I've never held back in showing my love. What's more, I've never expected some sort of payback or reward for all my grand gestures. I just like seeing the people around me happy. However, when you pair a passionate heart, unapologetically chaotic energy, and grade school, you're gonna get a bumpy ride.

The first time I felt like I was "too much" was in third grade, when I was told by a classmate that my recess hopscotch buddy didn't like me because I talked too much. And remember my ex-best friend? I'll never forget the day she asked me to dress better for church because I embarrassed her with my eccentric getups (e.g., a pink leopard-print matching set!). In middle school, when I started experimenting with head-wrap styles, I'd get asked if it was a costume and be snickered at in the hallways. A few times, I even noticed teachers stop calling on me in class, usually after I excitedly connected a topic to a Black issue I was thinking about.

Although experiences like these never fully stopped me from expressing myself, I remember slowly becoming quieter in school, trying to make as little commotion in class as possible, and generally attempting to dial myself down so I would never be "too much" for other people. By the time I finished my first and only season of middle school basketball and was awarded a jar of gum for being "bubbly," I realized I'd probably never be able to run away from what made me *me*. Still, my first year of high school felt like an unending game of hide-and-shrink as I tried my best to fit in and not ruffle feathers with my personality.

Because I was younger, and especially because I was a young Black girl, I assumed that it was my responsibility to break myself into bite-size pieces for other people's comfort. That's part of the reason I connect so much with Maya Angelou. Like Maya, I made a habit of shutting up parts of myself that I deemed unacceptable or ugly, even if they were just parts of my identity.

As I grew older, I found a friend group that felt like a breath of fresh air. When I first met them, I saw how they bounced off the walls as much as I did. They were loud with their emotions, just as I longed to be again, and they showered me with love the way I'd done in earlier friendships. In their embrace, I felt emboldened to set my heart flying free.

The more I was with people who had the courage to show themselves honestly, the more my fear of abandonment waned. But had my friends never been themselves with me, I'd never have had the courage to do the same. I learned that when you *don't* hold back how you express love, you can encourage others to love themselves. That understanding became more precious to me than fitting into other people's comfort zones.

I knew I still had work to do in shedding my anxiety over being myself, so I started filming my own pep talk videos every morning. I set up my phone and spoke love over myself the way I would for my friends, and watched the videos back later. I talked like I was writing myself a letter, hyped myself up, and made sure that even if no one else accepted and enjoyed my heart, *I* would. Someone might say throwing it back on camera while shouting, "You're enough!" just to make yourself laugh is "too much," but I say it's the perfect concoction to restore faith in your chaotic energy.

Eventually, I started posting my personal pep talks online, and after a few weeks they started going viral, reaching people all over the world. I've received the sweetest messages from people about how these pep talks have changed their perspectives on life—and for some, even contributed to saving their lives.

In the rest of this chapter, watch what happens when Maya Angelou learns to stop limiting herself and unleash her full energy into the world. And remember that letting yourself be "too much" too can actually open up a life that is too *little*.

A woman named Mrs. Flowers walks into Maya's grandmother's general store. She walks with such grace that to Maya it feels like a gift just to look upon her. She buys a couple things, but before leaving she asks Maya to help carry her bags home. The two of them stroll down the road back to the woman's house. There, Mrs. Flowers gives Maya cookies, books, and a set of directions: to memorize poetry, to read novels aloud to herself, and to *never* mistreat a book.

That was the first of many visits. Over the next few years Mrs. Flowers supplied Maya with poetry and literature and made her feel seen and valued. Mrs. Flowers didn't just give Maya cookies and stories; she challenged her often to speak. In an NPR interview, Maya said that one day Mrs. Flowers asked her, "Do you love poetry?" Instead of speaking, Maya wrote "yes" on a tablet she carried around. Mrs. Flowers answered, "You do not love poetry. You will never love it until you speak it. Until it comes across your tongue, through your teeth, over your lips, you will never love poetry." Maya ran out of the house, thinking, *I'll never go back there again.* Then Mrs. Flowers said, "Welp, I tried!" and never talked to Maya again.

Taylor, please be for real.

Ahhh, you know me well, reader—but let's think about this situation! At this point, Maya hadn't been speaking for years, not even to her family. If I were Mrs. Flowers, I would have had some serious doubts about pushing Maya any further. But Mrs. Flowers believed in Maya. She saw that the seed of Maya's voice just needed consistent encouragement to help with the harrowing task of breaking through the soil. Mrs. Flowers didn't back down and instead continued to be exactly who she was—which was exactly what Maya needed. Maya did come back to Mrs. Flowers's house, again and again. And over time she started to open up. When she was thirteen, she started reciting poetry out loud.

What a brave girl Maya was! After years of hiding herself from the world, she opened up again, even without the certainty that things would turn out okay. With Mrs. Flowers's help, Maya planted her *own* seed of hope: the knowledge that even when it was scary, she still had the power to fully embrace her story, her voice, and every part of herself, so that she could live a life full of love. In doing so, she let that seed sprout and start the journey to becoming a full-grown tree.

The rest of Maya's path through life wasn't without pain. She faced losses, trauma, and difficult decisions she could never have predicted. But the one thing that remained consistent in her life was her voice. She had once associated her gift of speech, writing, and expression with death, but it was the very thing that brought her the essence of life. Without Mrs. Flowers encouraging her to water that seed, Maya would have never toured the world, written her own award-winning literature, or moved masses to better their own lives just by reciting her own poetry.

Mrs. Flowers shared her deep love of poetry, which pushed Maya to live in a more passionate, outspoken way herself. Decades later, Maya's love for life encouraged me to embrace my own chaotic energy as a teenager—and so did every friend who, like Mrs. Flowers did for Maya, shared their own "too much" moments with me and showed me it was okay to be wholly and completely myself.

Now I'm sharing my chaotic energy and my love with you.

Remember that every little thing about you is a breath of fresh air for someone. Your quirks are the intricate engravings of your identity. When you show up unapologetically with them, like Maya Angelou did, they may be "too much" for some—but they could also be key to changing the lives of many.

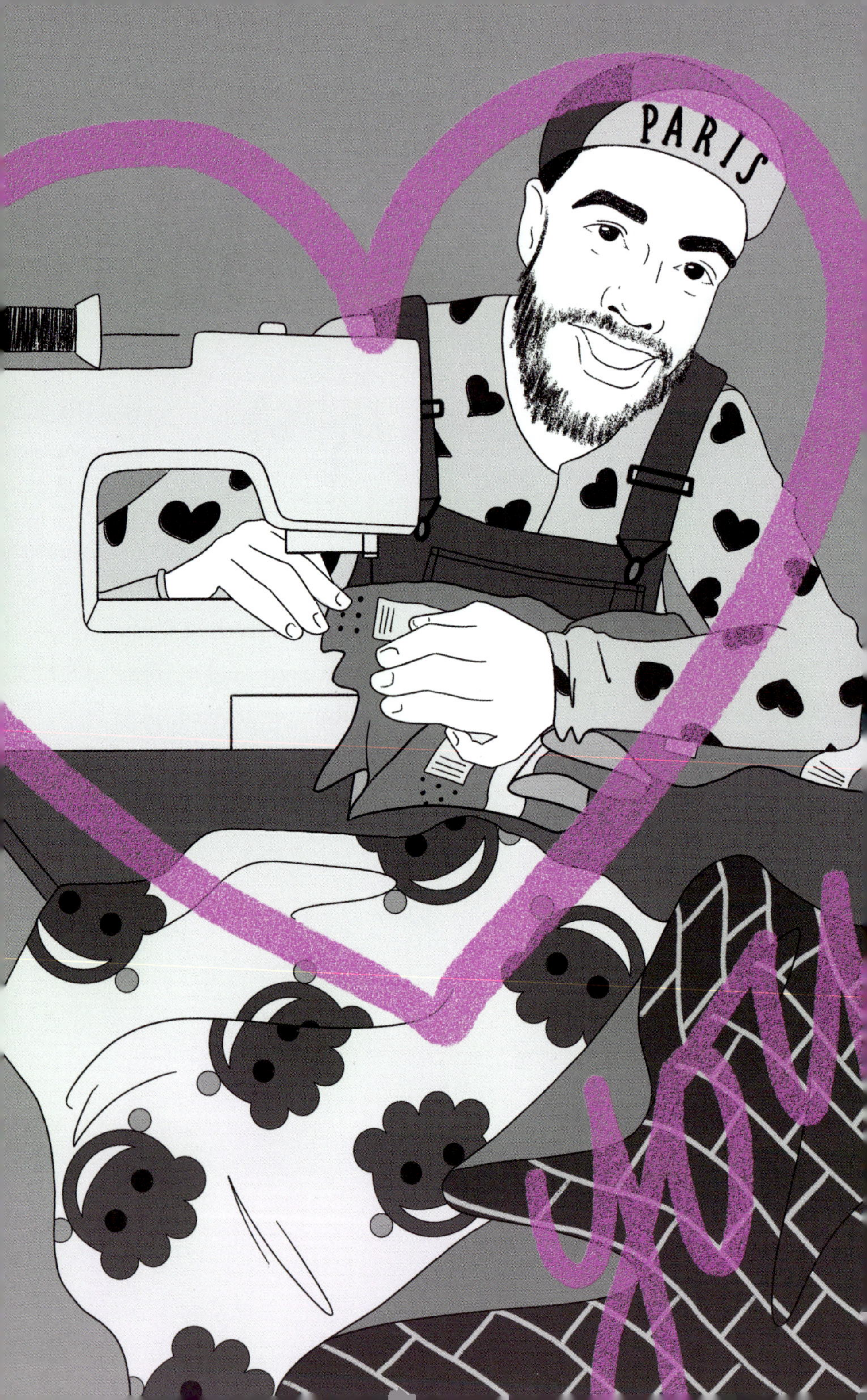
PARIS

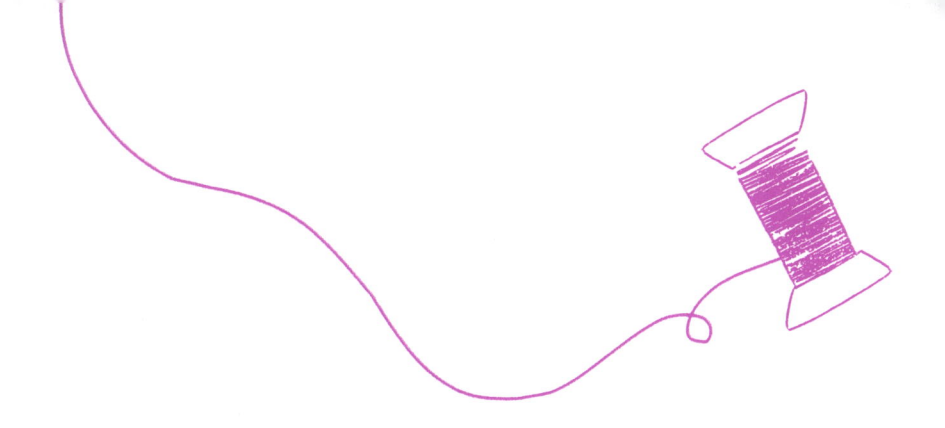

PATRICK KELLY
AND HOW REJECTION CAN BECOME REDIRECTION

WHAT SONG ARE YOU LISTENING TO RIGHT NOW?
For me, Stevie Wonder is currently singing that he's "signed, sealed, and delivered." Speaking of dope book-reading playlists, I can definitely see Patrick Kelly playing Stevie Wonder at one of his fabulous Paris fashion shows in the eighties. Can you imagine sitting in the front row, ready to see the season's newest designs, and the DJ is in the back spinning your favorite boujee auntie's playlist? I'd end up jumping on the runway to start a *Soul Train* line with the models!

That kind of fun, infectious energy was Patrick Kelly's goal as a fashion designer. By using his platform to spread a message of joy, love, and community, he became a high-profile icon in Paris. You know that one friend whose smile fills the room with sunshine, who makes you feel like it's Christmas morning? That was the way Patrick Kelly walked through life.

Patrick was born in 1954, and before he was a high-fashion success, he grew up in segregated Mississippi. As a boy, he was surrounded by style thanks to the Southern women in his life, especially his grandmother. He admired her Sunday-best outfits—and the magazines she'd bring home from work, filled with the latest fashions. One day, as little Patrick watched his grandmother flip through the magazines, he noticed the absence of Black women in their pages. A light sparked in Patrick's young mind, and from then on, his heart would be set on fashion with a purpose.

Once Patrick grew older and learned how to sew from his aunt, he left his hometown for Atlanta, with dreams of working in fashion. His most notable job at the beginning of his journey? Dressing mannequins for window displays at an Yves Saint Laurent boutique. If you didn't grow up watching *Project Runway* with your mom while finishing your math homework and you don't know who Yves Saint Laurent is, I'll put it this way: the designer label Yves Saint Laurent is like an infinity stone in the gauntlet of designer brands.

I can imagine Patrick having so much fun weaving his own personal style with the signature Yves Saint Laurent look. Even though he worked at a luxury label, I think the coolest part about this time in Patrick's life was the vintage upcycling business he ran, cutting and sewing together vintage designer dresses to create unique Patrick Kelly masterpieces.

What was a Patrick Kelly masterpiece, you ask? For me, every Patrick Kelly creation looks like I'd find it in a closet in my dreams. Not in a "this is my one and only fantasy dress" kind of way—more like "How did I end up with a dress that literally makes me look like the Eiffel Tower, headpiece included?" Patrick Kelly designed with whimsy in mind, and his signature touch was always buttons, in an homage to the mismatched buttons his grandmother would use to fix his clothing when he was a little boy.

Patrick's business selling vintage clothes and designing his own dresses led him to open a store in Atlanta, participate in local fashion shows, and meet up-and-coming Black models. (Side note: I would have loved to be one of those models wearing Patrick Kelly's early designs. In elementary school, I used to dress to the nines no matter where I went, hoping Tyra Banks would suddenly appear and whisk me away to become America's next top model. Even though that never happened, no one could tell me I shouldn't rock my pink ruffled skirt, light-up shoes, zebra shirt, and sparkly hat to the nearest 7-Eleven. Why *shouldn't* I practice my strut while getting a cherry Slurpee? The world is your runway—so walk it!)

With more and more models flocking to Patrick Kelly, it was clear to him that he should upgrade his fashion aspirations to his next stop: New York City. Patrick got himself together. He made the arrangements, thought about all the designs he'd create to shake up New York, and practiced the victory dance he'd do when Elaine Welteroth announced that he'd won *Project Runway*. (Okay, maybe he was about twenty-five years too early to be dreaming about being on *Project Runway*, but I bet he did all the other stuff!)

So Patrick Kelly went to New York, a major fashion hub, and received a scholarship to attend Parsons School of Design! However, things began to crumble when he found out the scholarship had been taken back.

What do you mean "taken back"? What could Patrick have done to make them do that?

It's not a matter of what Patrick did, so much as who he was. As Bjorn Amelan, Patrick's future partner, told a reporter at *Vice* magazine, "Once the dean of Parsons discovered that Patrick Kelly wasn't an Irishman, he refused to give him the scholarship." Like many colleges during that time, refusing admission to students of color was the norm, and Patrick was no exception.

No worries though, our guy knew how to find the fashion world wherever he went. He did it growing up with his grandmother, and again in Atlanta with his clothing store, so he could do it in the Big Apple too! All he had to do was bring his honest self and style to fashion brands and work his way up. So Patrick began designing portfolios customized to different brands and fashion houses in New York, blending his voice with the companies'. There's no doubt that he poured all his heart, time, and energy into these designs.

You know the feeling *right* before you go onstage to perform, start the first play of a sports game, or hear the teacher's "begin" in a timed test? Those nerves about putting all you've rehearsed and practiced on the line are no joke! So you can imagine how much excitement and anticipation Patrick must have had, walking into these fashion houses with his portfolio to try to get an interview for whatever positions they had open.

I can picture it: Patrick walks through the gold revolving doors of a tall skyscraper in his best-dressed outfit with an accessory he designed himself. In his arms he carries a folder of sketches, ready to impress the designers he'd moved all the way from Atlanta to work with. With his head held high and a loving smile on his face, he approaches the receptionist counter. But before he can ask what floor he should go to for an interview, the receptionist blurts out, "The service elevator is in the back," without even looking him in the eye. When he clarifies his desire for a job in fashion, the receptionist finally looks up, taking in Patrick and his appearance, and with an edge to her voice replies, "Not likely."

Patrick was rejected and denied by brand after brand. I particularly admire this part of Patrick Kelly's story because it shows how much audacity and bravery it took him just to continue being himself. He moved from a familiar place in Atlanta to highly competitive New York not even twenty years after the Civil Rights Act of 1964. On top of that, he sought a career in a notoriously exclusive, White, and rigid industry: fashion. Patrick grew up with segregation in Mississippi, so he'd seen how discrimination directly affected his family's lives—and his own. When it came to recognizing his own worth, he had already learned that he couldn't measure by how often people said no or underestimated him. He kept trying to find a fashion job in New York for an entire year. And it. Was. Exhausting. He made friends there, but money and employment were hard to come by. It seemed as though New York had chewed him up and spit him out. Yet through it all, Patrick continued designing, sewing, and creating.

What would you do if you'd been rejected just for being your true self?

TAYSTORY!

It's so exciting to be a content creator on social media! Since I started working as one professionally, I've experienced things I'd only daydreamed about before, like collaborating with my favorite creators, getting free stuff from brands, and going to fun parties and events. One of the most common questions I've gotten from kids I've met is: "Do any celebrities follow you?" And I feel *so* cool saying yes. (Shonda Rhimes, if you're reading this, I'd be so good in *Bridgerton*. I'll even learn to do a British accent!)

The highs of being a content creator are amazing—but the lows can feel like absolute failure because the scale for success is so black-and-white. Fame has become a defining characteristic of being an "influencer" and having a career in social media. The consensus is that if your videos are going viral online, that means you are doing something right. But if they are falling into the shadows with only a few likes and shares, sorry! You just don't have that *it* factor. Though I haven't been a creator for as long as others, I have thoroughly learned that while it can be a glamorous occupation, it's also a fertile ground for imposter syndrome and seeking validation from others.

After my first video went viral when I was seventeen, my brain started deciding whether or not I was a good creator based on how well my content performed online and how many opportunities I received. For the next couple of years, I struggled with my self-worth whenever a Black history video would tank in views compared to the last one I posted. It hurt because I poured my heart into every video, but I didn't receive the applause every time. When I saw my social media mutuals get invited to influencer parties, or get brand deals, I'd beat myself up for not getting the opportunity too. Because a big part of being in social media is who you know, I thought that if I wasn't going to parties, I was no one, and nobody wanted to know me. And when I *did* go to parties, I had some unpleasant experiences talking to influencers who immediately abandoned our conversation when someone more famous walked in.

Put all that together and you get a recipe for self-esteem issues. *Yay! Self-Loathing Soup!*

I was so scared of failing as a creator and losing everything I'd been blessed with, and because the only tools for success I'd seen people use were fame and recognition, that became my standard. A couple years after I first started going viral, my view count was slowly going down and I was seeing less traction on my videos, even when I started changing their style to try to fit what other people's viral content was doing. Pretty soon, I started to question whether my education videos were even valuable anymore, and how qualified I was to create them.

Cue the record scratch. SCREEECH. I was *still* a very successful creator who was consistently working and who continued to see amazing growth! But the power of comparison is sneakier than a Foot Locker sale before a track meet, and it blinded me to the reason I started making videos in the first place.

It *was* true that I was falling out of the level of popularity I'd had when I first started posting, and it *was* true that my content was less trendy, but I took that information and let it spoil what being creative meant to me. Every loss or rejection overshadowed my wins and chipped away at my motivation to create. The cherry on top was not being invited to VidCon, an IRL convention for online creators. I'd been invited the year before, but because of missed deadlines and rescheduling, I hadn't been able to go. I tried to play it off and be grateful that I was ever invited in the first place, but that voice of comparison wouldn't stop saying things like, "If only you had more views. If only you'd made better videos. If only you were a more entertaining person. If only you were like the others."

Oddly enough, the revelation that redirected my thinking came from a K-Drama. Here's an entry from my diary during that time:

> 3/11/22
>
> There is a character in a K-drama I'm watching named Na Hee-do. There are characteristics about her which I deeply admire. Her story begins with people saying she is a fencing prodigy. As she gets older, her skill seems to halt. As more people stop supporting her, opportunities are taken, and she continues to lose matches, her sense of drive, purpose, and complete LOVE for the sport persists.
>
> I bring this up because today I realized part of me has been fighting not for purpose, but for respect. I've been afraid this whole

time that someone would look at me and think I'm nothing. That I won't amount to anything . . . but instead of other routes . . . I've been thinking the route to that is fame. I don't blame myself, but I won't let it continue. VidCon cut me from their featured creators. I won't be attending anymore. When I found out I felt heavy rejection. Heavy senses of insecurity. But as Mom talked to me she told me these things which I believe God spoke through her: "This door is closing for a reason. God has something to replace this that is better for you. A queen isn't defined by what happens to her, but how she reacts to it."

At that moment I thought, what did Na Hee-do do when she lost anything? I remembered how she never took it as a loss, but simply enjoyed the process of her passion and the contentment of knowing she worked hard. When I think about it, there are still many things I want to do in my life and if I continue chasing quick industry respect, I'll never grow respect for myself. I want to live and know I worked hard. God has graced and trusted me with a platform, money,

> and opportunity. And I refuse to let it spoil my character, intentions, and desires simply because it offers an easier path. I didn't sign up for ease. I signed up to serve. As I watch all my friends head to VidCon this year, I will cheer them on wholeheartedly. I will release my jealousy and accept faith and resolve.

Now that I've grown, I see so many ways I could call my past self spoiled and out of touch for being so deeply affected by superficial things like views, likes, and event invites. Instead, I know that this just shows how much I cared about doing my best in my new profession, and I see how much working through those emotions strengthened me.

When I decided likes and views would no longer have a large influence in determining my worth, I made space in my mind for new standards of success and ended up building my unique perspective even more. I learned that rejection can be tough to face, but it can also be a sign that you've outgrown something and that it's time to level up. I remember sitting down and completely reworking the way I filmed content, beefing up my production and dedicating more time to research. My standard became the quality of my art and how it could encourage others, not how well it would do in an algorithm. Not every video went viral, and for a while my views decreased even more, but I was

> building a reputation of excellence and craftsmanship that distinguished my videos for anyone who saw them.
>
> Months later, that redirection showed me a new path when I found out I'd been cast in *Nick News*, a TV show on Nickelodeon that reports news for kids. When the team described their reasons for choosing me, they brought up many educational videos I'd made that had "flopped" on TikTok but showed the drive they were looking for. I moved to a new place in my career, and doing so didn't take copying other people or going even more viral than I had before; it took keeping my faith in who I was and taking rejection as a redirection.

Patrick was sick of New York, and it felt like New York was sick of him. He faced rejection after rejection, and it seemed like the more he poured himself into his fashion, the more it was overlooked. If it were me, I'd heavily consider booking the cheapest and fastest ticket back to Atlanta, where I felt I had a chance. I wouldn't have blamed Patrick if that was on his mind too, but without as many opportunities to show off and profit from his skills as he'd had in Atlanta, the problem was his wallet. Money was tight and his predicament felt bleak.

One of the only comforts Patrick had in New York was the friends around him, including one whom he confided in about his struggles, his rejections, his dreams for success, and his desire to leave New York: Pat Cleveland. Pat was an influential supermodel, and when she heard about Patrick's troubles, she knew her next move. She bought him a first-class ticket to Paris.

What I love about Pat and Patrick's friendship is her strong belief in his potential. Although Patrick's career felt at a standstill in New York, she was willing to see him through the downs and use her own success to bring him up with her. That's a true friend!

Paris felt like putting on a custom-fitted Cult Gaia dress that hugs you just right. Although Patrick still found himself selling his creations on the street, he arrived with enough contacts to also get a job designing and sewing costumes for the dancers at Le Palace, one of the most popular clubs in the city. One of his signature designs was a simple dress made from a tube of jersey knit fabric, adorned with those same mismatched buttons. People started noticing his designs all over Paris, including Françoise Chassagnac, who placed Patrick's creations in Victoire, a hot Paris boutique. Patrick was on his *way*! Little did Paris know, the luxurious designer dresses they were wearing were sewn in Patrick's hotel room.

If you want to get an idea of how these dresses came together, here's an unofficial guide to making a Patrick Kelly–inspired dress:

1. Find solid-colored, stretchy fabric of your choice.

2. Fold the fabric hamburger-style so that there are two layers.

3. Lay a tank top in your size over the fold of the

fabric, trace an outline around it slightly wider than the tank top (as seen below), and extend the bottom of the outline to the length you'd like the dress to be.

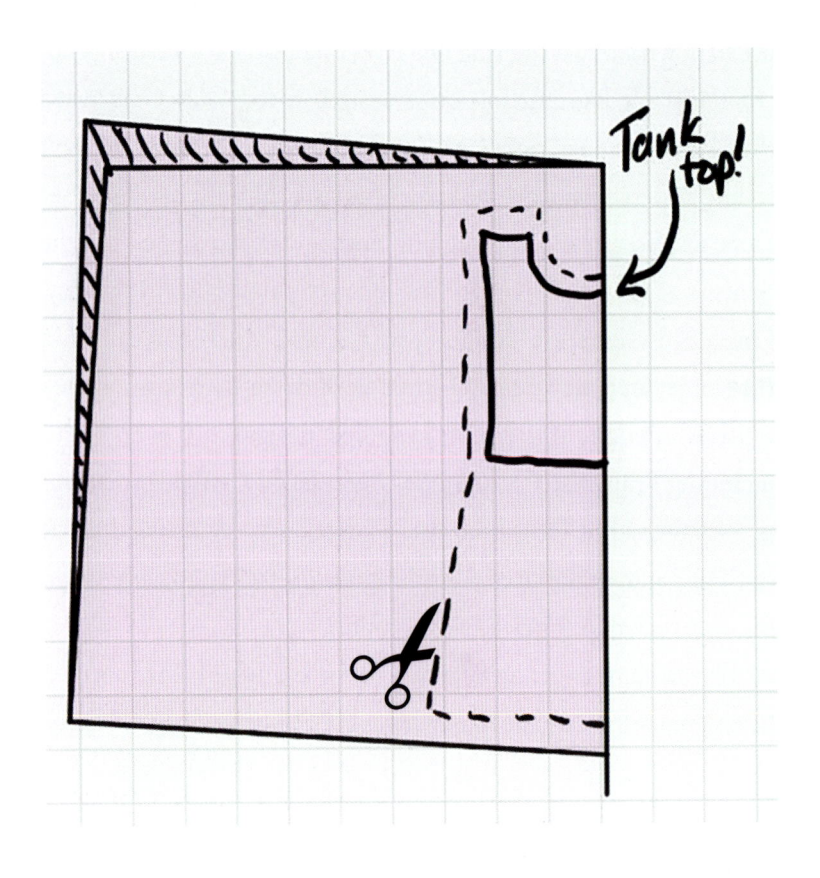

4. Cut along the outline. (Don't cut on the fold!) Repeat steps one to four so you have two pieces.

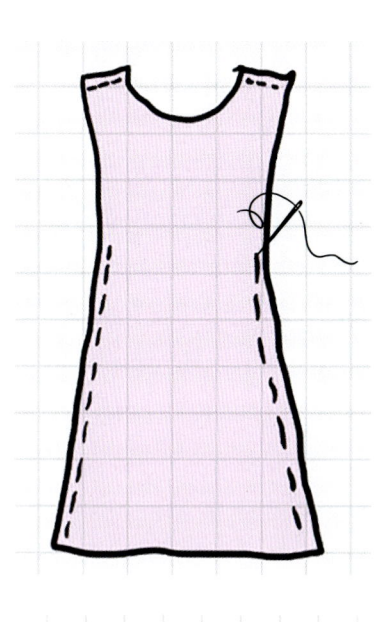

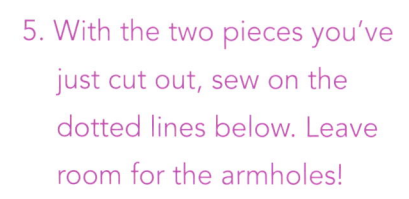

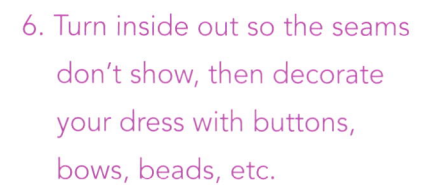

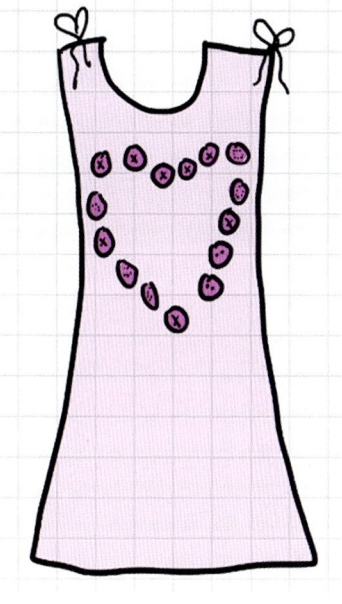

5. With the two pieces you've just cut out, sew on the dotted lines below. Leave room for the armholes!

6. Turn inside out so the seams don't show, then decorate your dress with buttons, bows, beads, etc.

7. Turn your school hallway into a *runway* and strut in your dress while listening to "Alien Superstar" by Beyoncé. (Mandatory step.)

Patrick Kelly's name was in Paris's mouth, and French *Elle* magazine hit him up to feature his designs in a *six-page spread*! You know who was picking up their phone to order a dress and get Patrick a bag? *Everybody and they mama!* Paris fell in love with Patrick, and everyone he encountered felt his personality radiate around them. Françoise Chassagnac, the buyer who put Patrick's dresses in Victoire boutiques, later told *Vice*, "Patrick was charismatic, and his dresses were elegant, colorful, funny, and unpretentious." Patrick Kelly's brand was *hot*. He made his way into magazines, had his designs all over Paris, and dressed celebrities like Iman, Cicely Tyson (our fashion icon!), and Madonna. He was so loved that he became the first American designer to be added into the Chambre Syndicale du Prêt-à-Porter, which is like an extremely exclusive fashion club for brands like Dior, Yves Saint Laurent, and Chanel.

With this new platform, Patrick turned Paris into his own personal playground for fun and made the city a hub for Black models. When a Black model would come to Paris, they knew they'd have a home with Patrick Kelly. Patrick would invite big groups over and cook greens, grits, and fried chicken, providing everyone with the comfort and acceptance New York hadn't offered him. In a world that tried to dim his light, his best revenge was doubling his love.

Before each of Patrick's shows, he'd make an appearance. He'd come out on the runway in his iconic overalls and colorful hat, waving to the attendees. He'd pull out a can of red spray paint and color a BIG heart below his brand logo with a cursive "you" next to it. Then the show would start. Bright, patterned, colorful designs walked down the runway, and all of them looked *amazing*. A few looks you'd see if you were at one of his shows (all based on actual Patrick Kelly clothes!): A model wears a suit with playing dice printed all over it, plus a coordinating headpiece with two massive dice on it. Behind her is Grace Jones in a black leotard covered in embellishments over red stockings; the long pieces of multicolored fabric attached to the leotard drape around her knees. Another model walks down in a romantic black dress with kissy lips all over the bodice, with a giant set of kissy lips as a headpiece. Patrick's fashion represented the joy of life, and his goal was to design clothes that, in his words, "make you smile."

Another well-known design Patrick used was an image reminiscent of the golliwog.

A golly . . . what?

Remember when I told you about minstrel shows? Imagine the blackface those performers would use, but as a cartoon character. That's a golliwog. The golliwog cartoon image was invented in England in 1895, and it caught on in the segregated South, too. The golliwog was all over the place for decades. There were golliwog figurines, dolls, apparel, and advertisements. The golliwog's face usually looked like a black or dark brown circle with two beady eyes, a big, wide smile with cherry-red lips, and curly tufts of hair on top. For me, looking at a golliwog makes me think of discrimination and stereotypes. My mind immediately goes to painful stories of Black people's struggles and the degradation of their beauty. It reminds me that many view Black beauty not as elegance but as comedy.

That's why it surprised me at first to see that Patrick used his own version of a golliwog in many of his garment prints. In fact, that image became the official logo of his name brand. Patrick grew up in segregated Mississippi and had faced struggles with racism himself, so why would he place this racist symbol on his clothes? Then I read a story Patrick told the *Washington Post* about an interaction he had at an airport, which shifted things into perspective for me. In his hand, Patrick carried a Black doll that a friend had just given him. A Black woman approached him to ask about it, but she also shared with Patrick that her daughter would never want a Black doll. Taken aback, he said, "If your daughter would throw away a Black doll and she's Black there is something wrong."

Patrick snatched the insult thrown at his community in the form of the golliwog and shoved it back in the face of racism as if to say, "Ha! This belongs to *me* now. You can no longer use it to hurt me!" He dug his hands into dirty mud so he could pull out the gold it covered up. He made what the world deemed the lowest bar of beauty into *high fashion*. Patrick Kelly's reclaimed version of the golliwog has the same basic design as one made for the purpose of exploiting Black people, but it carries an entirely different spirit and intention: *love and beauty*. Regardless of anyone's thoughts on Patrick Kelly's use of this symbol, I believe that in every part of his life, he saw rejection and darkness as things that could be redirected and transformed into warm light.

Patrick Kelly passed away when he was only thirty-six years old after complications from AIDS, but he left behind a trail of sunshine in his fashion and the way he brought people together. His resolve to stay himself through rejection paved the way for future Black designers like Kerby Jean-Raymond of Pyer Moss,

Virgil Abloh of Off-White, Kimora Lee Simmons of Baby Phat, and more.

Next time you take an L, remember Patrick Kelly's story and ask yourself: What values did I learn from this? Have my goals or dreams changed? Am I stronger now? How can I turn this around for my good? In your life, you can take defeats and see them as fresh opportunities to walk victoriously toward the destiny you're meant to thrive in.

And when you walk, make sure to strut.

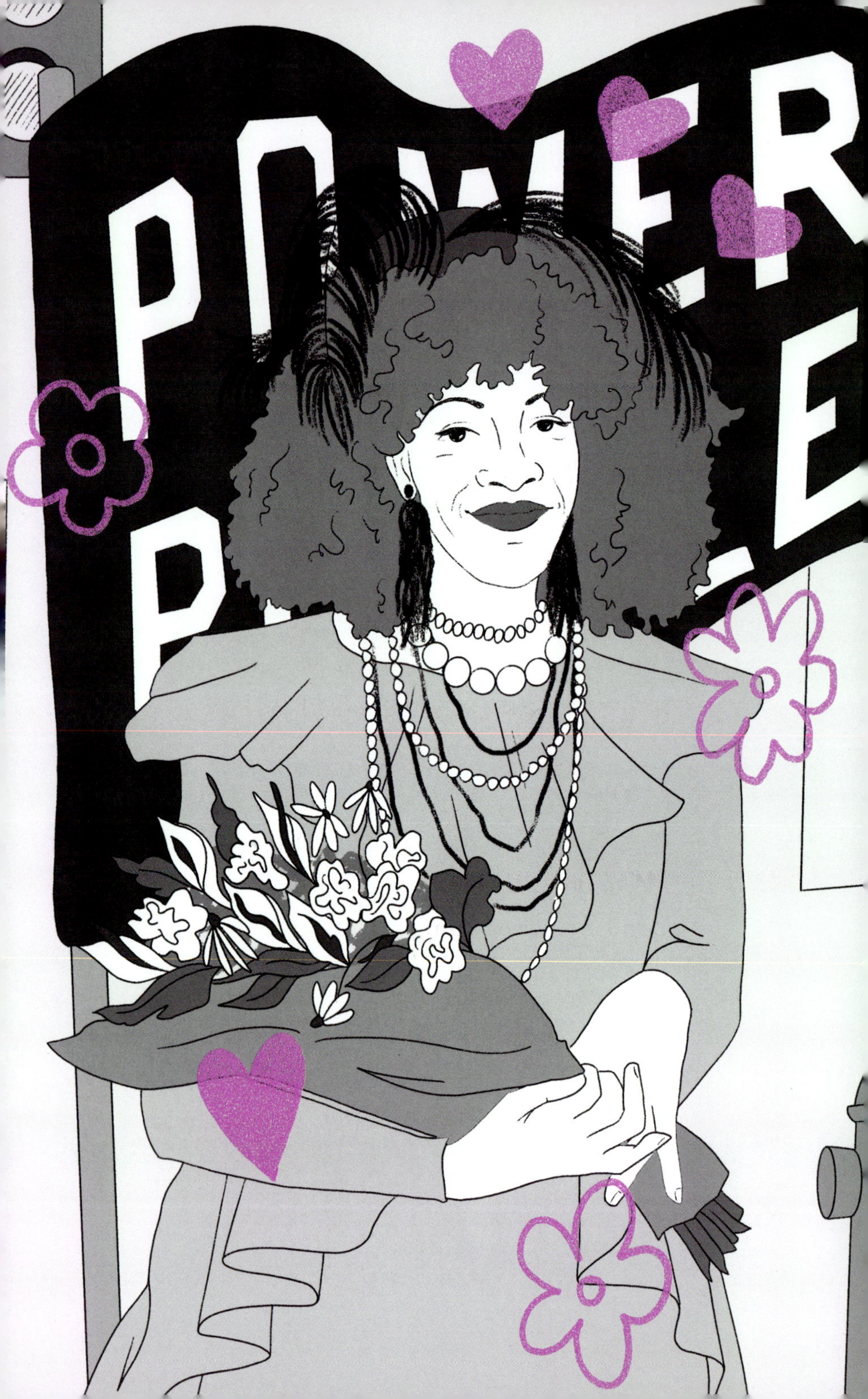

Disclaimer: From the research I've done, Marsha P. Johnson never clearly expressed a specific gender identity and went by both she/her and he/him pronouns in different situations. For the sake of this chapter's consistency, I'll be sticking to she/her pronouns, which Marsha used most of the time.

MARSHA P. JOHNSON
AND WHY ANGER IS NOT AN ENEMY

WAIT!

This chapter includes discussion of Black trauma and violence. Read at your own risk—or if you need to, go ahead and skip this chapter. No hard feelings! We all must protect our joy sometimes.

WHAT MAKES YOU MAD? LIKE, REALLY MAD? LIKE "a non-skippable ad coming up right in the middle of a good YouTube video" kind of mad? For me, I feel the most anger when I'm misunderstood—and mistreated because of it. It's like when that one kid is bothering you in class, and no matter what you say or do, they disregard your feelings and refuse to leave you alone. Feeling angry and ignored when you express that anger is frustrating! When anger comes up, it might feel like you should push it down and fight it off at all costs, but our next figure, Marsha P. Johnson, proves that this doesn't have to be the case.

Marsha P. Johnson had incredible tenacity, becoming one of the driving forces behind the 1970s and eighties American gay rights movement and spending her life advocating for the well-being of queer youth. She moved through life with a generosity of heart that made people who knew her describe her as an angel or a saint. However, what moves me most about Marsha is how she accomplished incredible things when she saw her anger not as an enemy but as fuel to create change.

Marsha was born in New Jersey in 1945 and raised in a religious household. She started trying on dresses around age five, but because she was assigned male at birth (meaning the doctor said, "it's a boy"), her parents were not pleased about this. Dresses felt right to Marsha. They made her happy. However, Marsha's parents and the community around her believed that she should stop wearing dresses and only act how they believed a boy "should" act. That meant goodbye beautiful ruffles and twirly skirts, hello boring, plain khakis. Still, as Marsha grew older, it was apparent she wouldn't be conforming to what society pressured her to be anytime soon.

Pause. Taylor, I'm a little lost. Can you explain all that a bit more?

Sure. Let's break it down!

Marsha grew up in a society where things like wearing dresses and putting on makeup were forms of gender identity expression strictly for women. From a young age, Marsha naturally gravitated toward these things. When she wore them, they made her feel strong and confident. And the more she learned about herself, the more she realized that some things her society required of "boys" didn't align with what she thought of herself. The things that men around her wore as their form of gender identity expression felt mismatched for Marsha. This didn't mean she was wrong or needed fixing; it just meant her heart called her in a different direction.

Cultures around the world have all kinds of traditional expressions of gender. For example, Indonesia, Scotland, and Fiji all have types of skirts that are worn by anyone, no matter their gender identity! So your definition of a "man" or "woman" might be completely different from someone else's.

It's safe to say that clothes don't define a person's gender; their heart does. In the words of genderqueer writer and filmmaker Stuart Getty in their book *How to They/Them*, "Gender identity is about feeling your body, knowing what's right, and following your own guidance. This doesn't just apply to gender-neutral folks; this means being a woman however you want to be a woman and being a man however you want to be a man."

Now, if I were to go up to someone in the 1940s and say something like "gender identity," they might react the same way a Victorian-era child would if I gave them one of those Blue Heat–flavored Takis chips (I don't know *how* y'all eat those): confused and offended. If open discussions about gender expression are just now becoming more common in the US, you can imagine how difficult it was to express anything other than what society expected in Marsha's time. There were many laws based on the idea that being gay or stepping outside the strict rules of gender in any way was evil. If you openly expressed your identity and stood proud in who you were, but that didn't line up with what people thought you *should* be, you could get arrested—or worse. By owning her queerness and femininity while also being Black, Marsha was taking an even bigger risk than a White queer person. When she turned seventeen and decided to move to New York City, the road was bound to be tough.

Marsha came to the city with only fifteen dollars and a bag of clothes. Although she was homeless for a time, she'd walk New York dressed in brightly colored thrift-store dresses and accessories made from things she found on the street or in the trash. Her signature look included beautifully arranged flower crowns that she made herself. She often had flowers given to her by vendors who let her sleep under the tables they arranged bouquets on.

Marsha's personality matched the bright colors in her outfits. She was outgoing, energetic, and generous. Though she usually needed money herself, she was the kind of person who'd give her last few dollars to someone else who was struggling. This kindness became intertwined with how many viewed Marsha P. Johnson, and she survived by forming friendships with other people who'd also left their homes for New York, to live lives where they could be free to be themselves. With her new community, she participated in drag shows and was a member of a drag queen group called Hot Peaches that performed regularly around the city. Soon those around her began to see her as someone who brought sunshine and charisma wherever she went.

But even if Marsha arrived in New York with nothing but honesty and open arms, the city was stubborn in accepting her embrace. Many people appreciated Marsha's confidence and good aura, but some within the gay community also rejected her for the way she dressed. Even at gay bars, Marsha was sometimes thrown out because they didn't want people there who dressed outside the gender norm. In a time when Black and LGBTQ+ people had very few places they could be themselves, Marsha had even fewer than most. But even still, she wouldn't give up her identity for other people's comfort. She was harassed by police and often arrested for wearing makeup in public. After one arrest, a judge asked Marsha what the *P* in her name stood for, and she famously responded by raising her arm, snapping in the air, and confidently declaring, "Pay It No Mind," in response to people questioning her gender expression—aka one of the best self-introductions in history.

Marsha P. Johnson lived how people are often afraid to live: by bravely accepting all of who she was and refusing to change for others. That gave her the ability to offer goodness to the world, but the world didn't want it. She had little money, few safe spaces, and frequent problems with police who wanted to punish her for living out loud. I don't know about you, but constantly examining and defending my right to exist, just for others to misunderstand my pain, would make me furious—and rightfully so. As positive and kind as Marsha was, she was no exception to feeling the buildup of anger that many of us experience when we are mistreated. In Marsha's case, this was a daily battle that took a heavy toll on her over time. Friends of Marsha's remember her struggling with mental illness, as well as moments where she lashed out physically at people who harassed her.

Whoa. That's a serious kind of anger.

You're right, reader! And Marsha thought so, too! She didn't like getting into fights, but when all other forms of communication and self-defense seem to do you no good, it can feel like violence is the only option. I can already see posters in the school hallway that say *Violence is never the answer*. And while I agree, I also have to add that violence stemming from anger is a serious sign that something is way past due for change. Once Marsha recognized that sign, she wouldn't ignore it.

TAYSTORY!

Let's play rock, paper, scissors. Ready . . . Rock, paper, scissors, **GO!**

HA! I won.

Do you feel a little like you just played a game of chance

that was rigged against you? That's what it felt like to live with an old roommate of mine. Every day it would be *so fun* wondering whether she'd be nice like paper, ignore me for no good reason like rock, or slam doors and shoot sharp looks at me like scissors. Given that our college twin beds were less than three feet apart from each other, it was really hard to separate myself from her when she was in a mood.

I tried my hardest to be nice to her. I listened to her rant about her classes, gave advice when she asked for help with a problem, and didn't comment on the weekly phone calls with her parents where she'd scream at them at the top of her lungs. I didn't complain about her keeping her lamp on and loudly gaming on her computer till three a.m. every night, or about her refusal to take out the trash or do her share of cleaning the bathroom. But none of this stopped *her* from having a venomous attitude when I had my music up a little too high during the day, or from asking me to spray Lysol on her mail before I handed it to her. UGH! #lawdhelpme

What hammered the nail in the coffin of our potential friendship was when she confronted me about how distant I'd been, a few weeks into the semester. She stopped me one day before heading to class and asked if something was wrong or if she'd done something to upset me. In an admittedly condescending tone, I explained that parts of her personality were harsh to me and the way she talked to her parents made me uncomfortable, and I told her not to be surprised if I continued keeping my distance.

Taylor! That was so rude!

I agree, reader! What I should have done was be up-front with my feelings from the start, even if she disagreed with me, and find compromises to address the problems she had the capacity to change. Instead of confronting her and setting clear boundaries, I went inside myself and shut her out. I thought that if I threw out hints that I didn't want to be around her, she'd see my discomfort and magically become self-aware enough to change her behavior. But staying quiet only let anger grow in me, and my poor communication resulted in an outburst and an awkward situation with my roommate.

When I said all this to her, she was visibly upset and left. When she came back, it was radio silence. She walked past me like I didn't exist. Let me tell you: ignoring someone in a small dorm room takes *persistence*. Do you know how awkward it is to do that weird dance when you need to get past someone in a tight space while also giving them the silent treatment?

I felt terrible. I asked her if we could talk and apologized for how I handled the situation. I said how sorry I was for keeping her in the dark about my discomfort and apologized for judging her so harshly. In my head, I felt relief. We could finally move on and maybe even be cool! But instead, she said we would have *serious* problems if I talked badly about her parents again.

Whoa . . . how did we get here? Did we skip a few chapters or what?

I apologized! I hadn't even insulted her parents! I did all the steps of handling things healthily and laying down my ego, so weren't we supposed to make up and move forward?

Nope. After that conversation, we simply stopped speaking to each other unless it was necessary.

Even though my interactions with my roommate made me feel anger like I hadn't felt in years (I made a playlist called "Teeth Chattering Mad" for moments I needed to let off steam!), I didn't do much to improve my living situation. Instead, I found myself endlessly complaining about her to my friends. When they'd give me suggestions, like moving out, involving an RA, or (probably the most creative one) framing her for pulling the fire alarm, I'd always find an excuse to instead do nothing.

I tried my best to ignore the anger and resentment simmering in the room every day, thinking that avoiding our problems would make it easier to get through the year. Spoiler alert: it did not. In our last week of living together, nothing had been resolved, we had another big fight, and I left for home feeling stressed. When I reflect on that year now, I shake my head at how much mental energy I spent ignoring or criticizing my rage rather than listening to it.

> There were reasonable actions I could have taken to improve my living situation, but I thought that acting on my anger and irritation in any way made me immature and weak. I didn't realize that anger was my mind's way of telling me that, by ignoring my own needs and forcing myself to stay somewhere I didn't want to be, I was mistreating myself.
>
> If I were to talk to past-Taylor from that time, I'd tell her that I might have gained a better understanding of my roommate—and discovered things I needed to grow in, too—if I'd let my anger evolve into productive action. I would tell her that anger is a valid emotion, one that deserves just as much of a voice as joy. It's from anger that we learn the edge of our boundaries, and what's necessary to protect them! Since then, I've learned that anger doesn't define who we are—and that, as Marsha P. Johnson reminds me, it's the actions we take as a result that show us who we can be

One of the hangout spots that did let Marsha enter was the Stonewall Inn. It was and still is a popular gay bar on Christopher Street, and in 1969, it became a landmark in the fight for gay rights. At that time, the police would often raid gay bars and arrest people, and the Stonewall Inn was no different. The police had been paying visits—and let's just say they were not showing up to sing Diana Ross karaoke.

One night when Marsha arrived, she saw police lining

people up for arrest, roughing them up, and throwing them out of the bar. Frustrated, people gathered outside to shout and protest the police, who continued to harass bar patrons. I can imagine Marsha standing there remembering all the times she was arrested and thrown out of bars herself. I imagine her anger rising as she reflected on all the moments when society had treated her and her friends like they had no right to exist unless they were invisible. But tonight, invisible would be the last word to describe Marsha P. Johnson. Legend says that Marsha was the one who started the riot, but according to multiple sources cited in *Pay It No Mind*, a 2012 documentary about her life, she joined the struggle after it was already underway by throwing a glass into a mirror, shouting, "I got my civil rights!"

From that moment on, Marsha was pivotal in the following six-day rebellion against police called the Stonewall Uprising. Remember the feeling of someone mistreating you in class? This rebellion was a reaction to decades of mistreatment of LGBTQ+ people. It wasn't the first gay rights protest, but it gained a lot of public attention and was certainly a turning point—and Marsha, along with her friend and fellow activist Sylvia Rivera, led much of the rebellion. They made their frustrations, anger, and calls for civil rights visible to the entire nation.

Marsha and Sylvia were both key figures in keeping up the momentum of the gay rights movement. Together, they advocated for inclusion of transgender people in the fight for gay rights. At one of the first gay pride parades, the organizers attempted to ban drag queens from walking. Marsha heard this and, like her name, paid it no mind. The day of the parade, she and other queens jumped in, leading the parade from front and center. *Iconic!* Another way Marsha and Sylvia amplified the voices of trans people was through STAR, a program created to help house young transgender and gender nonconforming people living on the streets. Their program reached multiple cities and further put the spotlight on LGBTQ+ rights and struggles.

As Marsha became a more and more prominent face in the fight for gay rights, people saw her smile, her warm demeanor, and her signature flowers on her head, and they didn't only see her as a symbol for gay rights. She also served as a reminder of all the Black and brown people who for decades had been mistreated the most while also *doing* the most to push the gay rights movement forward.

In 1992, when Marsha was only forty-six, her body was found in the Hudson River. Many of Marsha's friends say she was murdered, but the police ruled it a suicide with a lackluster investigation. At her funeral, hundreds of people attended, standing outside on the street when the church became full. In 2012, after years of controversy, the police officially reopened Marsha's case, though it still has never been solved.

The fight for gay and trans rights is nowhere near over today, but I wish Marsha could see the incredible people carrying on her mission—and how instrumental she was in the progress that's been made. Today, Marsha is glorified for her effervescence and praised for doing necessary work to help LGBTQ+ people live more freely. I admire her, because when Marsha was angry, she didn't question the validity of her feelings. She gave her anger attention, letting it direct her to become a more effective leader. She's taught me that anger doesn't have to be an enemy: it can be the starting point in changing everything for the better.

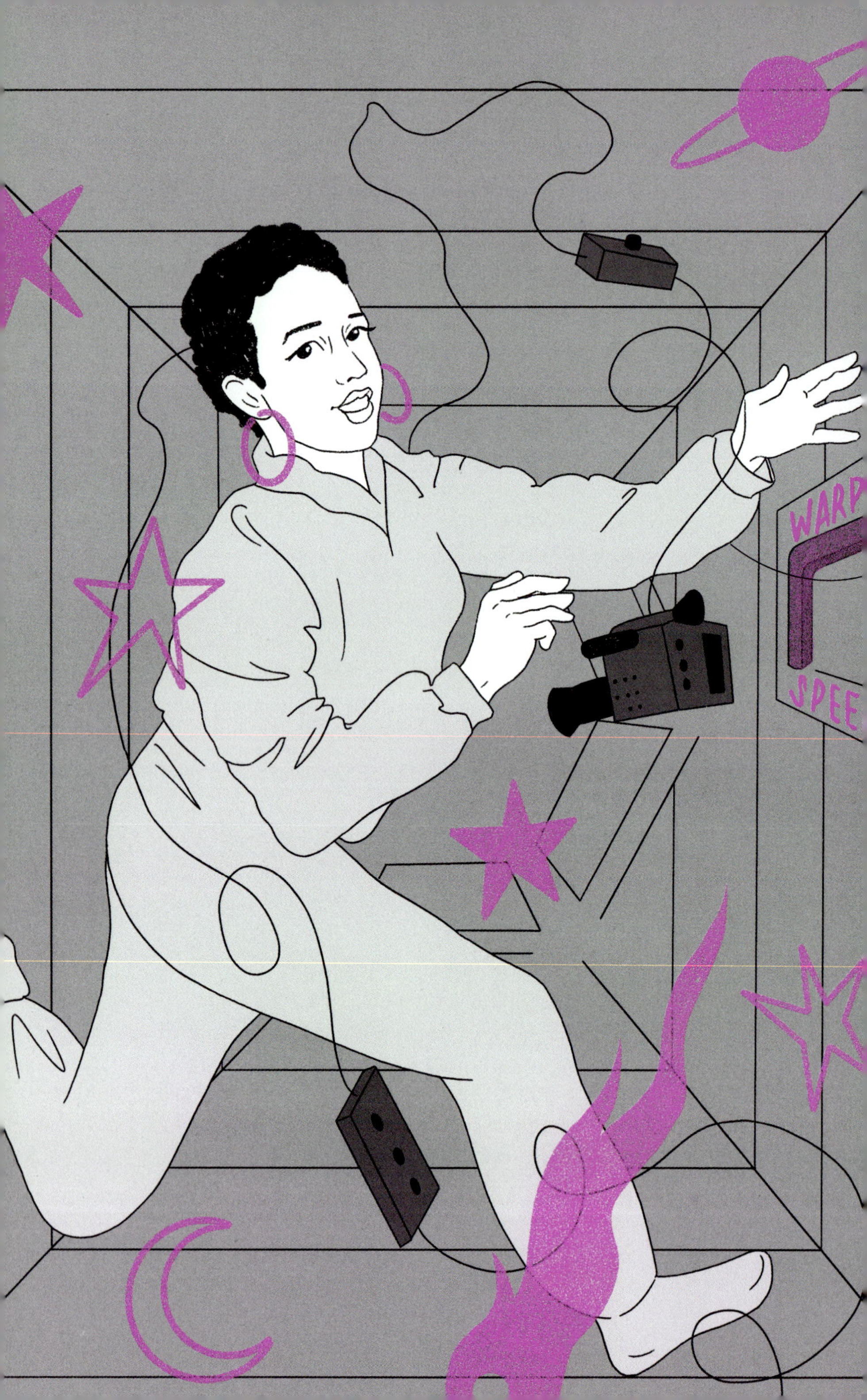
WARP
SPEE

MAE JEMISON
AND HOW DREAMING BIG WILL HELP YOU REACH THE STARS

THERE ARE TWO THINGS I'M DEATHLY AFRAID OF: the deep sea and space. There are *so many* things about both that we don't know. Have you *seen* what those fish look like down where the sun doesn't reach the ocean? If someone invited me to go see them in person, I'd block them and throw away my phone so they'd never find me again. As for space, watching the *Gravity* trailer when I was little was enough to make me content just looking at the moon and never imagining myself in any spaceship ever.

The biggest reason for my aversion to these things is fear of the unknown. Entering a space I've never been in before without guidelines on how to survive sends shivers down my spine. *Especially* if the things in that space (like big fish monsters) might have a mission to hurt me. If things go badly, I hate the idea of not knowing what to do and not having control.

If you've ever had to be "the new kid" at school or give a public speech in front of a big crowd, this kind of fear is probably familiar to you—and you probably also know how much hope and audacity you need to persist when you aren't sure how things will turn out. Someone who took persistence to another level was Mae Jemison, the first Black woman in the United States to become an astronaut and visit outer space. Today lots of kids want to become astronauts when they grow up (maybe you do too!), but for a Black girl growing up in the 1960s, going to space wasn't so easy to dream about. Let's picture it. . . .

In her pajamas, curled up close to the television, preteen Mae's eyes were glued to the screen. Aside from dance lessons, learning about science, and tuning in to NASA's *Apollo* spaceship takeoffs, Mae's favorite pastime was imagining herself as Lieutenant Uhura, the stylish *Star Trek* crewmember played by actress Nichelle Nichols. With each episode, Mae fell more in love with Lieutenant Uhura's assertiveness and strength in her leadership role on the spaceship. Most importantly, Lieutenant Uhura was a Black woman. Because of this, Mae could see *herself* traveling through a universe of stars and planets too. (The power of representation!)

Even as a young girl, Mae could sense a difference between the imaginary world of *Star Trek* and the very real limitations of the world she lived in. Mae grew up during some of the most pivotal moments of the civil rights movement—but even though the barriers that were being broken opened up a bigger range of careers and opportunities for Black people, it was still rare to see people of color with jobs in STEM.

This didn't stop Mae from dreaming, though. I can imagine her conversations with adults at the cookout each year:

Auntie: Hey, lil Mae, whatcha been doing lately?
Mae: Watching *Star Trek*.
Auntie: Ooh! Looks like we got a future actress! Do you want to be like Cicely Tyson and be on TV?
Mae: I'm going to go to high school early and then go to college early and then I'm going to become a scientist and go into space like Lieutenant Uhura, in that order, Auntie.
Auntie: Uh . . . huh . . . sure thing, baby.

People around Mae probably had a lot of doubts about her aspirations. Guess how many astronauts of color were at NASA when Mae was little? Zero! Guess how many *women* were astronauts at NASA when Mae was little? Zero! On top of this, some civil rights activists protested against space exploration, saying the money used to land on the moon should have been used to improve conditions in Black neighborhoods on Earth instead. As you can imagine, becoming an astronaut was not a common dream for Black people. Even when Mae Jemison told her kindergarten teacher that she wanted to be a scientist, she shared in a 1992 *Ebony* magazine interview that the teacher responded, "Don't you mean a nurse?" To me, this feels like a flashback to that Halloween in preschool when I spent the entire day telling people that my crown and dress did *not* make me a princess—I was a *queen*!

Despite other people's doubts, Mae kept her word, entering high school at twelve and going to Stanford University at sixteen to study chemical engineering. With her head held high, she walked into her first college classes, focused on her dream. As the days went by, though, Mae quickly noticed the lack of . . . *seasoning* in the room with her. Class by class, a feeling of "otherness" from the Stanford students and teachers crept in. Stanford wasn't exactly known for having an abundance of diversity; in 1960, only a decade prior to Mae's attendance, they'd had two Black students in the entire freshman class. In an interview with the *Washington Post*, Mae said, "Stanford was the best school I could have gone to, and I had ran into some wonderful professors there in the sciences, as well. But the overall feel was, hmm, should you be here?"

Having attended schools and been in classes where I was often the only Black student myself, I can imagine some experiences Mae probably had: students taking seats far away to avoid you, months going by without teachers learning your name (or worse, confusing it with another Black student's), unfounded and hurtful jokes about your appearance, and being ignored by teachers when raising your hand or requesting leadership positions. Not only was Mae one of few Black students in her classes, she was also younger than everyone else. By the numbers, she was not a typical Stanford student.

To get the education she desired so deeply, Mae had to face the unknown *every day*. Would she feel accepted by her classmates today? What if a professor said something condescending? What if she couldn't do well enough to meet everyone's standards? If I were Mae, those would be fears I'd have. So how did she get through it?

Her answer in that *Washington Post* interview was that "some arrogance is necessary for women and minorities to be successful in a White male–dominated society." For me, that translates to: "When you enter a space, you must be the biggest believer in your own worth to succeed." Even if Mae was nervous or afraid, she knew exactly what she wanted *and* believed she deserved it. Channeling Lieutenant Uhura's perseverance and strength, Mae worked her way through school and earned bachelor's degrees in both chemical engineering and African and Afro-American studies (shout-out to Black history buffs!).

Over the next chapter of her life, Mae achieved her childhood dream of working in the STEM fields. While in medical school at Cornell, Mae spent time in Cuba doing medical research and in Thailand working at a Cambodian refugee camp. After Cornell, she joined the Peace Corps as a medical officer and managed their healthcare programs in West Africa. Two years later, she returned to the US and opened her own medical practice. She'd proven all her naysayers wrong and done everything she'd set out to do!

Well . . . not everything. In 1983, Mae heard about Sally

Ride, who took off in NASA's *Challenger* that year and became the first American woman to enter space. I can picture Mae watching the *Challenger*'s launch on television with the *Star Trek* theme playing in the back of her head. She'd beaten the odds and graduated from mostly White colleges; she'd built a science career in which she'd already done amazing work helping the world around her. Would Mae dare to let her dreams guide her yet again—this time to a space entirely outside her world, where no Black woman had gone before?

TAYSTORY!

One of my favorite Disney shows growing up was *Hannah Montana*. Missing an episode was as serious as a grandma missing one of her soap opera episodes (aka her "stories"). I loved the fact that Miley, the main character, could be a normal kid by day and a worldwide superstar by night. And *Hannah Montana* also gave me my first introduction to what working in the entertainment industry might be like. My family does not come from "the industry." Other than knowing that I might have to carry around a blond wig everywhere I went (and sing "The Best of Both Worlds" on command), I had no idea how the business of becoming a "celebrity" worked before I went viral online. That was a world I had never ever been close to before—but it was one I'd secretly always wanted to be part of. The closest I'd gotten was getting to watch my sister compete in *American Idol* when I was fifteen, but even then, I was just her cheerleader. I soon went back to regular life in the Midwest after she ended her time on the show.

As a kid, when I looked at the people around me, I quickly learned that my expected path after high school was to find a practical job and settle down in the same place I grew up. While that is a wonderful dream for many people, it just wasn't *mine*. I knew my whole life that I wanted to do something in the entertainment field. But for many people around me, making money with a creative job was like seeing a unicorn win homecoming queen. (Homecoming side note: I did once win homecoming queen by winning a dance battle at a school I didn't even attend!) In fifth grade, when I entered a writing competition for a national kids' magazine I loved, my friend even said to me point-blank, "Don't expect to win. Getting famous is one in a million." That was the mindset of many people around me: it's a one in a million chance, so why even try?

Thankfully, my parents, who'd given up dreams of their own because of the people they grew up with, continually encouraged my sister and me to pursue what our hearts really desired. So despite the doubts, I held on to my dream of working in a creative field—and when I went viral I *flipped out*! This was my opportunity to enter a space I'd always longed for. But as I grew and had success, I realized my world was about to open up in a very new way.

After graduating from the very real and not at all fake Hannah Montana How to Do Entertainment University, I'd learned the benefits of an agent and a manager to help me turn the art I was creating online into a real profession. After a few months, I signed with management and had a meeting with an agency. I felt on track and things were going well. I was proving people's expectations wrong! I was going to work in entertainment! But then, just as I was about to enter the agency meeting via Zoom, my throat started to choke up and my hands started to shake. I was *scared*. Suddenly, all those voices of doubt came back, and I thought that as soon as I opened my mouth, the big agency people would think, *Oh, she isn't what I thought. She's nobody.*

I was having a major case of imposter syndrome, which is when you feel a little like Hannah Montana—like you might look awesome on the outside, but your real unspecial self is undercover. For me, I had anxieties that someone might get too close and see that while I was *pretending* to be a smart, talented TikToker on the outside, inside I was actually lazy and unoriginal. Those negative things weren't true, but being the first person in my family (and community) to take a step like this made me question myself. If it was such a one in a million chance to follow your dreams, what made me believe I was good enough to even try? Why *me*?

So I went into the meeting super nervous. But it actually went amazingly well, and the team expressed how excited they were to start working with me.

Yay, Taylor, you did it! You must have been so happy!

Well, I was certainly relieved, but the anxiety from counting all the reasons I *shouldn't* have been in that meeting still weighed on me. When my sister asked how it went, I broke down in her arms. In just a few months, my entire life had been turned completely upside down—and while all my wildest dreams were coming true, I also had to start from square one, without a guidebook, because I'd never seen anyone else do this. I had to enter the unknown and face my fears of not being good enough, of failing, and of *losing it all* at just seventeen years old.

But as I've grown past that moment and walked into many more rooms with only a dream, I've learned that instead of asking "Why me?" I can tell myself, "This is for me." If I could talk to my younger self, I'd tell her: In every single place you go, hold your head up. Even if you're afraid of what might happen, you better walk in believing your worth is HIGH. Don't let anyone else's expectations about your journey stop you. When you believe in your own potential, others will too.

Two thousand applicants. Two thousand people put two thousand pens on two thousand pieces of paper and applied to be a part of NASA's astronaut program in 1987. And one of those pens belonged to Mae Jemison.

If I were Mae, I would not be able to *stand* the anticipation of waiting for an answer from NASA. And I would just *hate* if any interruptions happened in this book before *you* find out whether they accepted her—

TAYLOR'S 3 FUN SPACE PICKUP LINES!

1. When you leave me, I feel like the color of a sunset on Mars: blue.
2. You're like Venus: you're the hottest in my solar system.
3. The reasons I love you are like the number of stars in space: uncountable.

Yes, I learned those facts just for you, reader. I hope you're proud of me!

But Mae must have been even prouder of herself when she found out that her application had been *accepted*!! Bring out the galaxy greens, Big Bang banana pudding, and solar sweet tea 'cause we're having a cookout to celebrate! Along with fourteen other chosen applicants, Mae dedicated the next five years of her life to training to go to space.

Here's how I picture Mae on the day it was finally time to launch:

Mae sits in the space shuttle *Endeavor*, strapped in. She looks around at her fellow astronauts, at the rocket's controls and features, and hears mission control's countdown. *Five.* She thinks about the teachers who underestimated her. *Four.* All the unwelcoming treatment she pushed through at Stanford. *Three.* The friends and professors who uplifted her dreams. *Two.* Watching NASA's rocket launches as a girl. *One.* Watching Lieutenant Uhura. Her mouth curls into a giddy smile.

☆ BLAST OFF! ☆

Mae Jemison soared through the clouds, through Earth's atmosphere, and out into the galaxy. During her eight days in space, Mae carried a few special things with her: a banner for Alpha Kappa Alpha, the oldest sorority established by African American women; an Organization of African Unity flag; and proclamations from the DuSable Museum of African American History. She and the crew studied motion sickness, bone loss, and (my favorite) frog fertilization in space. If one of those frogs went back to the swamp after the trip, she probably would have described the trip as *ribbeting*.

Taylor, please just stick to the space jokes.

Hey, telling puns is not *comet-ing* a crime.

As soon as the spacecraft landed back on Earth, Mae was

pushed into the limelight. People started recognizing her in public, she was called to speak at schools and universities, and she was even inducted into the National Women's Hall of Fame. Now everyone believed Black women could be astronauts! In fact, the whole *world* collectively changed the picture of "space traveler" in their minds to Nichelle Nichols as Lieutenant Uhura!

Well, not quite. Even though Mae Jemison was living proof that people's idea of who could be an astronaut was too limited, she saw how easy it still was for some students to grow up thinking they didn't deserve to believe in their dreams, all because the people around them still made them feel like it was unattainable. Mae was determined to use her platform to encourage them. During a speech at her old high school, she told the students, "Sometimes people want to tell you to act or to be a certain way. Sometimes people want to limit you because of their own limited imaginations." When Mae's time at NASA came to an end, she created the Dorothy Jemison Foundation for Excellence, named after her mother. Through the foundation, she started a camp for twelve- to sixteen-year-olds called The Earth We Share to educate teens about science and technology.

As of this writing, Mae is still working as a scientist, and her work continues to open doors for *everyone* to explore their STEM dreams. But you know the real cherry on top? In 1993, Mae's inner child geeked out when she appeared in an episode of *Star Trek* and was visited on set by the very role model who led her to look to the stars: Nichelle Nichols. Mae was the first *real* astronaut to ever appear on the series!

Mae Jemison and her courage to enter a space full of unknowns, risky outcomes, and unwelcoming faces have taught me that, for our biggest dreams to come true, we must believe that we deserve the chance to make them happen. And moreover, once you see your desires come to pass, you have a responsibility to use that newfound power to make room for others like you to follow in your footsteps.

So: What will you do? What big dreams do you have? What spaces and rooms do you want to enter? When you feel afraid of the outcome, remember Mae's story and the stories of all the people I've told you about in this book. They have all been in your shoes, and because of their willingness to step into the unknown, they've opened up a path for you. Now the inspiration, power, and persistence from them lives inside you and has become your history.

Like all of them, you too have the ability to achieve your biggest dreams, despite any circumstance. Hold your head up high; you can't see the path to your greatness while looking down. If you walk through your life with curiosity, courage, and—most of all—the audacity to dream, be prepared . . .

To make history.

♥ TAYLOR

ACKNOWLEDGMENTS

I THANK GOD EVERY DAY FOR THE HONOR OF experiencing the people who are in my life. To Mom, Nana, Granddad, and all my family, thank you for teaching me the balance of having an openhearted and loving spirit and still not being afraid to kick someone to the curb. You have poured your all into me, and I pray to God every day He returns the goodness you gave to me tenfold. I love you. Christina, my older sister and match in life, thank you for having patience with me as I grow and being my hype woman. I look to you as an example of what it means to work hard and have the courage to grow graciously through pain.

To Stephanie, my superwoman of a manager, thank you for being my guide to what it means to be a professional in entertainment and giving me the confidence to jump headfirst into amazing new things (like writing a book!). To my literary agents, Sian-Ashleigh Edwards and Sabrina Taitz, y'all are incredible. You made me feel heard, seen, and encouraged to make this book exactly how I envisioned it. Thank you for bringing all of your passion and excitement to this book and having faith in me (and patience in waiting for me and deadlines to stop our feud and just hug it out). Thank you to Josh Upfal and Lauren Calza, my WME agents, and Eric Whitfield from my management, StayM88—you have been powerhouses and your support of my career has meant so much to me. Thank you to my editor, Sophia Jimenez. In addition to beautifully ironing out my writing and giving me direction in my jumble of ideas, thank you for being my guinea pig for my many puns and jokes. (You just get my humor. I love it.) Adriana Bellet, a huge thank-you for your artistry in visually capturing this book's energy and for making these figures look *beyond* cool. Oh, the woman you are! Karen Parker and Melissa Stuckey, thank you for your expertise and advice on making sure this book represented each figure honestly and honored their work and legacy. A huge thank-you to the Atheneum team—Feather Flores, Rebecca Syracuse, Irene Metaxatos, Hope Kim, Kaitlyn San Miguel, Tatyana Rosalia, and Jin Soo Chun—for fueling and believing in the mission behind this project.

To my friends who are real with me, have been my light

in frustration, and continue to be my rock in this journey, you mean so much to me and I love you. A big thank-you to the teachers and leaders who encouraged my dreams: Mr. Day, Toya Owens, Mr. and Mrs. Franklin, Mr. Bailey, Tandra Stewart, Mrs. Hall, and every educator I've had. You've prepared me to always learn, grow, and act in excellence.

To you, whether you're a follower, fan, or didn't know who I was before this book, thank you from the bottom of my heart for supporting what has always been and will continue to be my mission: to spread love, light, and growth. I would not be here without you, and I am grateful for you every day. You've changed my life forever.

ABOUT THE AUTHOR
(AKA MY EXCUSE TO BRAG)

TAYLOR CASSIDY is a content creator who gained popularity from her online series *Fast Black History*, where with quick wit and strong passion she teaches Black history to her audience of millions. She uses her platform to advocate for representation, education, and creativity. She earned a Creator Honor from Liza Koshy at the Streamy Awards for her online series *Black Girl Magic Minute* and spent three years as a host for Sirius XM's TikTok Radio channel. She's been featured on TikTok's Top 100 list under "Voices of Change: Most Impactful," *Teen Vogue*'s "21 Under 21" list, and *Forbes*'s "30 Under 30" list. In 2023, Taylor became an Emmy-nominated host for her work as a correspondent on Nickelodeon's *Nick News*, as well as the first-ever youth speaker at the United Nations' International Day of Remembrance of the Victims of Slavery and the Transatlantic Slave Trade. Generous with sharing motivation and good energy online, Taylor is passionate about encouraging others to dream bigger for themselves. She continues to use her platform to teach, spread joy, and share fun pictures of herself (like this one).

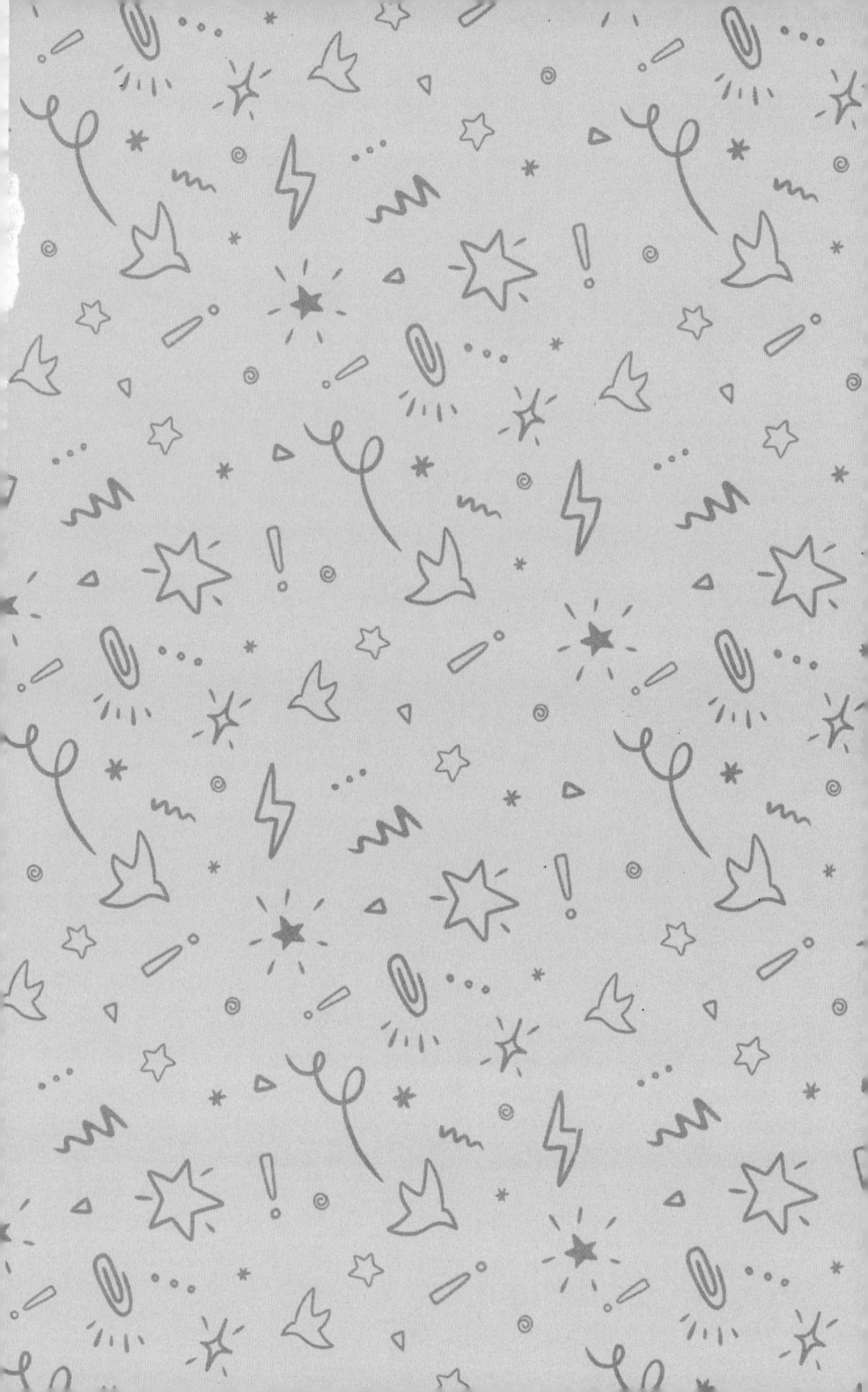

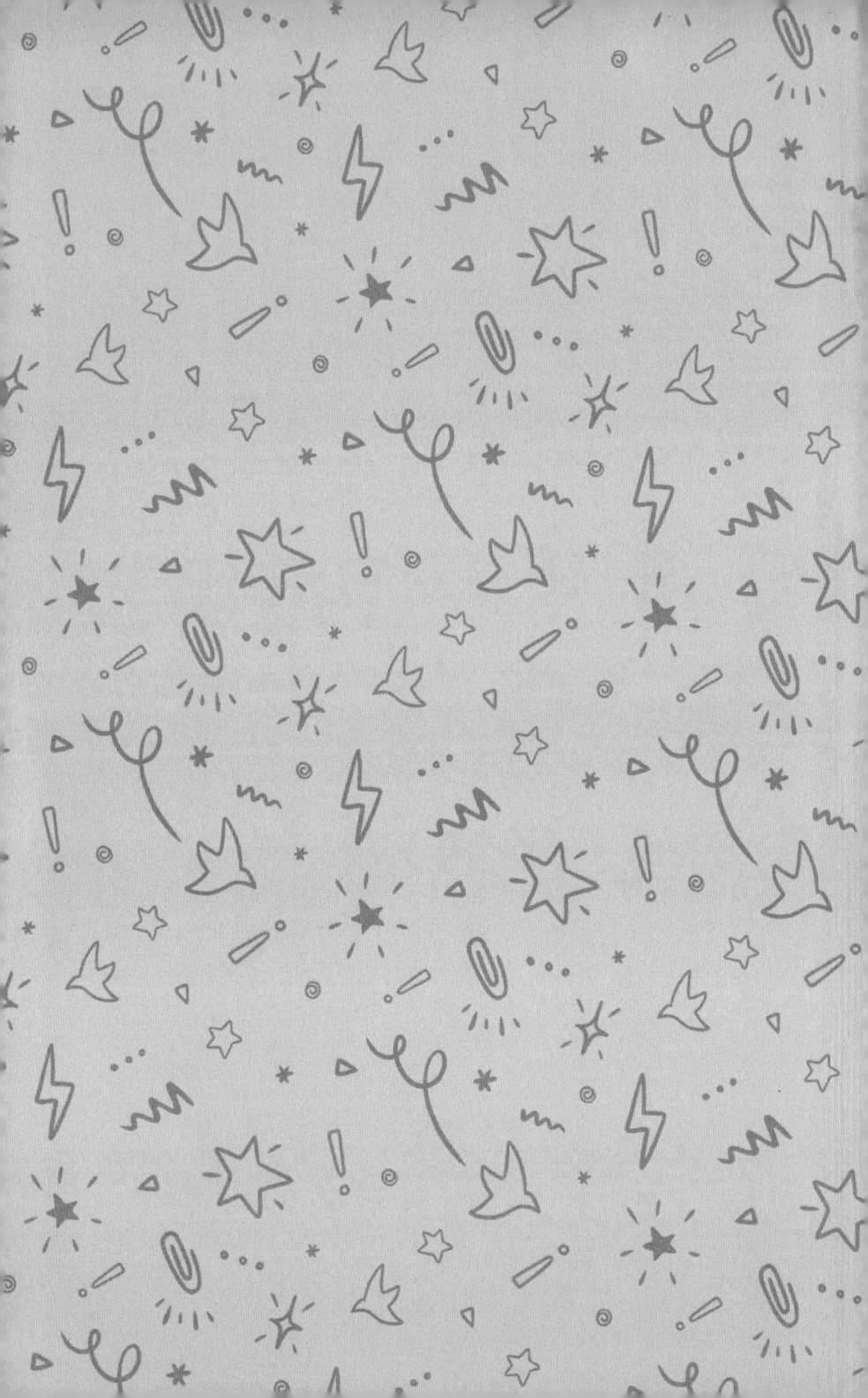